NATURAL LAW,
LAWS OF NATURE,
NATURAL RIGHTS

OTHER BOOKS BY FRANCIS OAKLEY

NATURAL LAW, LAWS OF NATURE, NATURAL RIGHTS

CONTINUITY AND DISCONTINUITY IN THE HISTORY OF IDEAS

FRANCIS OAKLEY

continuum

NEW YORK • LONDON

2005

The Continuum International Publishing Group Inc
15 East 26 Street, New York, NY 10010

The Continuum International Publishing Group Ltd
The Tower Building, 11 York Road, London SE1 7NX

www.continuumbooks.com

Library of Congress Cataloging-in-Publication Data
Oakley, Francis.
    Natural law, laws of nature, natural rights : continuity and
discontinuity in the history of ideas / Francis Oakley.
        p. cm.
    Includes bibliographical references and index.
    ISBN 0-8264-1765-5 (hardcover : alk. paper)
    1. Natural law – History.   I. Title.
K415.O553 2005
340′.112 – dc22
                                                            2005015096

MEMORIAE
A. P. d'ENTRÈVES
DOCTORIS

CONTENTS

PREFACE

Over the years, as the historiographic fortunes of intellectual history have risen and fallen only to rise again, I have found myself persistently drawn, less by any contrasuggestibility of temperament than by a sort of ineluctable fascination, to two abiding preoccupations. The first has been with the internal interconnections and affinities among ideas, their dynamism or "particular go" (Lovejoy's phrase),[1] and the logical pressures they are capable of exerting on the minds of those that think them. The second has been with the exploration of long-enduring intellectual traditions apt of their very nature to transgress not only disciplinary boundaries but also the chronological divisions that disciplinary training and historiographic tradition have made so prominent and obstructive a feature of the intellectual landscape. Neither preoccupation is altogether fashionable at the moment, though the growing prominence of the school of *Begriffsgeschichte* pioneered in Germany by Otto Brunner, Werner Conze, and Reinhart Koselleck, along with the recession in the Anglophone world of suspicions about the viability of the "influence model" as an explanatory tactic in the history of ideas, have both done something at least to fortify the epistemological confidence of those interested in the history of intellectual traditions.[2]

Whatever the case, the invitation extended to me to deliver the Merle Curti Lectures in intellectual history at the University of Wisconsin, Madison, in the autumn of 2001 afforded me the opportunity to pursue both preoccupations a little further via an exploration of the long tradition of discourse in the Western world concerning the complex of notions denoted by the terms natural law, laws of nature, natural rights. It also permitted me to share my preliminary conclusions with a gracious and sympathetic audience and, in response to the questions put to me, to clarify and sharpen their import. My visit to the campus and my encounter with Chadbourne Hall and Bascom Hill — both memorializing early presidents of the fledgling University of Wisconsin — also afforded me the opportunity to reflect on continuities and connections of a different type. For, like myself, John Bascom enjoyed the distinction of having spent several decades on our faculty here at Williams, and Paul Chadbourne is numbered among my predecessors in the post–Mark Hopkins presidential succession at the College. That sense of historic institutional connection, as well as the warm welcome extended to me by colleagues and friends at Madison, made my visit there both enjoyable and rewarding.

In that respect, I am particularly indebted to Thomas T. Spear, chair of the history department at Madison, and to three of his colleagues from whom, over the years, I have learned a great deal — my distinguished fellow medievalist, William J. Courtenay, and, from the early modern period into which, in hot pursuit of one idea or another, I have persistently been led to intrude, J. P. Somerville and Lee Palmer Wandel. Here at Williams, I am much indebted to my former colleague, Gary J. Jacobsohn, now of the University of Texas at Austin, for his kindness in giving the manuscript a critical reading, as also to my colleagues at the Oakley Center for the Humanities and Social Sciences with whom I was able to share drafts of a couple of these chapters. For their characteristically prompt work in preparing the manuscript for the press, I must also thank Donna Chenail and her fine staff in our faculty secretarial office.

In the course of revision for publication, these chapters have mutated from three into four. And if, as a medievalist, I regret the loss thereby of a measure of Trinitarian cachet, as one whose scholarly interests also impel him forward into the seventeenth and eighteenth centuries, I can only welcome the room for additional maneuver that has permitted me to focus more intently on the theory of natural rights and the intriguing *quaestio disputata* concerning its origins.

This book is dedicated to the memory of the late Alexander Passerin d'Entrèves, from whose characteristic kindness I benefited when I was starting out as a young member of the Yale History Department. A scholar with a long and generous intellectual reach, he had at one time or another, whether in Italy, England, or North America, taught literature and law as well as legal and political philosophy. But *Ideengeschichte*, he once told me, was the subject closest to his heart, and he had the distinction, certainly, of having focused attention on the development of the natural law tradition at a time when, in the Anglophone world at least, that was far from being a fashionable thing to do.

F. O.

Williamstown, Massachusetts
August 2004

One

METAPHYSICAL SCHEMATA AND INTELLECTUAL TRADITIONS

My concern in this book is with the complex of ideas clustered around the age-old notion of natural law as well as with particular instances of continuity and discontinuity to be found in the histories of those ideas. In approaching these matters, political philosophers have characteristically postulated (or simply assumed) the existence of a sharp discontinuity between modern natural law and natural rights thinking and the "classical," "Christian," and "medieval" natural law tradition taken to have preceded it. For those of warmly Straussian sympathies, indeed, the existence of such a sharp discontinuity appears to have been elevated to the status of a pivotal and unassailable article of faith, unresponsive to changes in the intellectual temperature and pressure and immune to the querulous caviling of historians. Not that historians themselves are necessarily prone to challenging that or other instances of claimed discontinuity. In relation to the history of ideas, indeed, concern with the *longue durée* — in this case with long-enduring patterns of thought — has for some years had something of an antiquated feel to it, whereas rupture, caesura, discontinuity, break have come to command a degree of attention bordering sometimes on the obsessive.

That is the case not only among those prone to resonating sympathetically to Michel Foucault's attempt to map in synchronic fashion the networks or grids of relationship that confer unity on the four great epistemes (or "epochs of epistemic coherence") into which he believes the years since the later Middle Ages have fallen, and to identify (though certainly not to explain) the stark discontinuities that he claims separated them from one another.[1] Even those whose thinking revolves within what are, by comparison at least, the more sublunary orbits of the Anglophone historiographic world are prone to giving short shrift to those preoccupied with such long-enduring patterns of thought. Arthur O. Lovejoy's classic *Great Chain of Being,* however much it was acclaimed when it first appeared over sixty years ago, is now, one cannot help feeling, dismissed more often than it is read. To Quentin Skinner, indeed, the Lovejovian project of concentrating on the idea itself as a unit and of tracing its morphology across long stretches of time is clearly misguided, wrong in principle, grounded in "a fundamental philosophical mistake." "My concern," he once famously proclaimed, "is not empirical but conceptual; not to insist that such histories can sometimes go wrong, but that they can never go right."[2] And if one shifts to an otherwise quite different point on the historiographic spectrum, to the late Lawrence Stone, who, after a moment of perhaps unwelcome epiphany on the road to the historiographic Damascus, had grudgingly conceded in the late 1970s that "quantification [had] not fulfilled the high hopes of twenty years [earlier]," that there might well be something, after all, to the efforts of the historians of ideas, that in the enterprise of historical explanation, then, "ideas, culture, and individual will" had now to be recognized as "independent variables" — if one shifts to Stone, even as he made those edifying though somewhat belated concessions, one finds that he still thought it necessary to insist that the very precondition for this novel interest, on the part of what he called "the new history," in trying to discover what was going on in people's heads in the past was nothing other than "the collapse of the traditional intellectual history treated as a kind of paper chase of ideas back through the ages" and usually ending up "with either Aristotle or Plato."[3] Concern with the *longue durée,* it seems, was still to lie under proscription, and if intellectual history was indeed to make a contribution (especially when it was concerned not with the beliefs, values, feelings, and attitudes of the inarticulate masses but with the ideas of elites), then those ideas could, profitably be studied only if the historian situated them precisely in the social, intellectual, and linguistic context of their specific era.

There is, of course, a good deal to be said about all of this, but it is not my intention to scratch that particular intellectual itch again on this particular occasion.[4] If I mention these things now, it is simply to provide a few historical coordinates or, if you wish, to situate contextually my own concern in what follows with the dialectic of continuity and discontinuity so evident in the ways in which, over the years, historians have attempted to come to terms with the more than two-thousand-year-old tradition of thinking — or, at least, tradition of discourse — to which the label "natural law thinking" has come to be attached. For in this particular connection, the interpretative price paid for either too casual (and universalizing) an assumption of continuity or too adamant (and provincializing) an insistence on discontinuity is, I believe, evident in unusual degree. What is called for is a careful and really quite delicate balance the principal features of which, focusing on what I believe to be a crucial period stretching from the fourteenth to the seventeenth centuries, it will be my purpose to achieve.

I

Of the divine right theory of kingship John Neville Figgis wrote, almost a century ago now and echoing the words of a distinguished contemporary, that "never has there been a doctrine better written *against* than the Divine Right of Kings."[5] Something similar could well be said about natural law thinking. Derided since the eighteenth century almost as often as it has been affirmed — and Jeremy Bentham's rejection of the affiliated doctrine of natural rights as "simple nonsense . . . , rhetorical nonsense, nonsense upon stilts"[6] is only the most celebrated of many such exercises in dismissal — its obituary has been published over the centuries with a degree of repetition no less misleading for being so reassuringly liturgical, not least of all, in recent years, by one of my distinguished predecessors in this Merle Curti lectureship. Writing in 1995 of the 1960s, and discussing the progressive replacement of "universalist" by "particularist" aspirations in the United States since World War II, as well as the concomitant "transition from species-centered to ethnos-centered discourse," David Hollinger observed that this transition "left academic leadership of the [universalist] resistance in the hands of dwindling cadres of Jesuits" and of those who followed Leo Strauss in his passionate defense of natural law.[7]

In times past, of course, Catholics themselves have sometimes proved reluctant about conceding any too easy or automatic an equation of Jesuit with Catholic. But if one forgets all of that and takes Hollinger really to have meant *Catholic* when he said *Jesuit,* then, looking back to the intellectual climate prevailing in the mid-twentieth century, there is of course something to the claim he was making.[8] And yet, as was so often the case at moments in the past when the demise of natural law theory had confidently been proclaimed, the obituary turns out, once more, to have been altogether too premature. The patient, indeed, had already been discharged from the hospital even before Hollinger chose to address the matter. Signs of recovery had become evident a full quarter of a century ago. By the late 1980s and early 1990s it was not uncommon, evoking such names as Germaine Grisez, Joseph Boyle, Robert George, Hadley Arkes, George Hittinger, Lloyd Weinreb, and, above all, John Finnis, to speak in terms of "a flowering of vital natural law philosophy" or of "a broad revival of interest in natural law theory among mainstream legal, political and moral philosophers," to comment, again, on "the richness of contemporary natural law theory," and to draw attention to the "remarkable assortment of natural law theories on offer in today's market-place of ideas" — "liberal" as well as "conservative," "substantive" no less than "procedural."[9]

Such unexpected manifestations of recovery parallel comparable pulses of revived vigor in the past, and it is perhaps because of such repeated evidences of enduring vitality that commentators have often been moved to affirm the extraordinary continuity across more than two millennia of the natural law tradition. They have done so, however, in ways that are more acceptable and less. To give an example of the type of affirmation of continuity that I myself would view as more acceptable, let me adduce the following from Paul Sigmund's little book *Natural Law in Political Thought*. Having prudently acknowledged the "bewildering variety of doctrines that have been associated with the term 'natural law'" and the concomitant degree of confusion surrounding its meaning, Sigmund nonetheless affirms that there would appear to be a continuing and

central assertion expressed or implied in most theories of natural law. This is the belief that there exists in nature and/or human nature a rational order which can provide intelligible value-statements independently of human will, that are universal in application, unchangeable in their ultimate content, and morally obligatory on mankind. These statements are expressed as laws or as moral imperatives which provide a basis for the evaluation of legal and political structures.[10]

Of course, it would be easy enough to criticize that formulation. It was written in 1971 and would probably be unacceptable to those who, since then, have framed deontological or, at least, nonconsequentialist theories of moral obligation rather than ontological theories of natural law, but who (Finnis quintessentially) have themselves been accused by other contemporary natural law theorists more traditional in their commitments of embracing, altogether too enthusiastically, "the characteristically modern ideal of metaphysical austerity," and even of attempting to frame a theory of "natural law without nature."[11] Sigmund's formulation, moreover, is also predicated upon an explicit embrace of the standard distancing of the juridical or moral and prescriptive notion of natural law from the scientific and descriptive concept of laws of physical nature which rose to such great prominence in the seventeenth century.[12] Commonplace enough that move may well be, but perhaps I should signal now that I will be urging later on that a certain interpretative price may well be paid for any too thoroughgoing or peremptory an insistence on that conceptual distinction.

All of that said, I believe it would be churlish to cavil too much at Sigmund's claim. Cutting through all the cautious qualifications and scholarly hesitations to which the sheer variety of natural law theories inevitably gives rise, it effectively catches the central intuition of the natural law tradition, namely, that human beings through the diligent use of their reason do have access to norms of justice that are in some profound sense natural and universal rather than conventional and provincial, and it explains the degree to which for long centuries in the past (as Hollinger clearly assumes) natural law was the principal carrier in the Western intellectual tradition of universalist or "species-centered" as opposed to "ethnos-centered" moral aspiration.[13] One can comfortably let it stand, then, as at least a useful provisional formulation.

The same, however, can hardly be said of the far more sweeping affirmations of a "perfectly continuous history" of natural law thinking to be found in so many a nineteenth- and twentieth-century history of political thought, and given classic and eloquent expression in the following statement made in 1948 by none other than Sir Ernest Barker, for some years the dean of those grand old historians who were still able and willing to take on the full sweep of European political thinking from classical Greeks to moderns. "The origin of the idea of natural law," he says,

> may be ascribed to an old and indefeasible movement of the human mind (we may trace it already to the *Antigone* of Sophocles) which impels it towards the notion of an eternal and immutable justice; a justice which human authority expresses, or ought to express — but does not make; a justice which human authority may fail to express — and must pay the penalty for failing to express by the diminution, or even the forfeiture, of its power to command. This justice is conceived as being the higher or ultimate law, proceeding from the nature of the universe — from the being of God and the reason of man. It follows that law — in the sense of the law of the last resort — is somehow above law-making. It follows that law makers, after all, are somehow under and subject to law. The movement of the mind of man towards these conceptions and their consequences [he goes

on] is already apparent in... Aristotle. But it was among the Stoic thinkers of the Hellenistic age that the movement first attained a large and general expression; and that expression... became a tradition of human civility which runs continuously from the [Stoics]... to the American **Revolution of 1776 and the French Revolution of 1789.** Allied to theology for many centuries — adopted by the Catholic Church, and forming part of the general teaching of the schoolmen and the canonists — the theory of Natural Law had become in the sixteenth century, and continued to remain during the seventeenth and the eighteenth, an independent and rationalist system, professed and expounded by the philosophers of the secular school of natural law.[14]

If that statement undoubtedly reflects a nobly coherent vision of the past, it is hardly a vision that corresponds to the somewhat gritty and certainly more baffling realities that one inevitably encounters if one resolutely resists succumbing to any sort of "fetishism of words"[15] and delves accordingly beneath the smooth patina of shared terminology. For while the persistence of such shared terminology does convey something of importance, it is necessary, I believe, to avoid confusing traditions merely "of argument or discourse," which imply no more minimally than "a shared subject matter" and center upon "a related set of questions or common concerns," with full-blown "traditions of thought" which, in responding to such questions and concerns, embody also a shared constellation of moral or metaphysical beliefs "and preserve across time a certain identity, continuity and authority."[16] If Barker's enduring natural law tradition of human civility may well qualify as a somewhat loose-limbed tradition of discourse, it certainly falls short of constituting anything as unified, coherent, or continuous as a single, discrete, tradition of thought. Soothing invocations of the authority of Thomas Aquinas notwithstanding, the currently fashionable form of natural law theorizing grounded (à la Finnis) in the postulation of a battery of self-evident "basic human goods" serving "as ultimate reasons for [moral] choice and action" has proved hard to harmonize with the more traditional Thomist or neo-Thomist ontologically grounded theories. Similarly, the early modern theorists associated with what Barker calls "the secular school of natural law" may stand at some distance from the natural law theorists of the Middle Ages. Certainly, the moderns themselves quite self-consciously believed that to be the case. It was Samuel Pufendorf, after all, who, in the late seventeenth century, lauded his immediate predecessor Hugo Grotius as the great innovator who had disentangled natural law from the toils of theological controversy, drawing it out from the long shadows cast by scholastic disputation into the clear light cast by the all-encompassing sun of reason.[17]

We ourselves will see that it would be unwise without severe qualification to accept that sweeping judgment of Pufendorf's, but it remains the case that until the very recent past most commentators took it at face value and saw Grotius as the figure responsible for breaking with what some refer to as "the classical Stoic and Christian [natural law] tradition," or "the classical and Scholastic Tradition of Natural Law,"[18] and for ushering in the development of a different and essentially modern tradition characterized by its secular, rationalistic, individualistic, and radical nature.[19]

But, then, to speak in one breath of the classical and Christian or even scholastic tradition of natural law thinking itself begs a whole multitude of questions. Commentators continue to wrangle about the propriety of seeking the roots of that tradition in the age of Hellenic classicism prior to the rise of Stoicism in the Hellenistic era. And the modernist perennially tempted to mistake the sometimes quite exceptional positions of Aquinas for *the* medieval view at large must be persuaded to acknowledge the fact that the long centuries customarily labeled as medieval harbored not one but multiple understandings of natural law. It is only, in fact, the conventional focus on the discontinuities between medieval and modern views that has served to project a spurious unity upon the disparate natural law theories current in the Middle Ages. Even if we ignore the differences between the views expressed by Stoic and patristic writers, or between patristic and juristic, or juristic and scholastic, or, among the jurists, between canonists and civilians — even if we do all of that and limit ourselves to the scholastic alone, the picture is by no means a simple one. Those commentators who in the past have talked so blithely about "the classical and Scholastic Tradition of Natural Law," or "the classical Stoic and Christian tradition," or "the grand Natural Law tradition of Cicero and the Schoolmen," or "the law of nature in classical and Christian sense," or even (thus Leo Strauss) "the natural right tradition" extending all the way from classical antiquity to its demise at the hands of Thomas Hobbes[20] — all of these have done so, I would suggest, because they have tended to assume that belief in the existence of a natural law necessarily presupposes a prior commitment to some form of ontological essentialism (or "realism," to use the term for it that medievals themselves somewhat confusingly employed).

Of course, if that assumption is prescriptively philosophical rather than descriptively historical, a case can be made for it, and such a case, certainly, has more than once been made.[21] But if the assumption is an historical one, it is indefensible — doubly unfortunate, indeed, in that it can lead one to conclude without further examination that the late medieval subscribers to one or other form of epistemological nominalism (as well as seventeenth-century successors like Hobbes and Locke) *could not* possibly have been natural law thinkers at all. Unhappily, it was common in the past to draw precisely that conclusion.[22] And yet it is a simple matter of fact that fourteenth- and fifteenth-century thinkers whom it is normal to classify at least loosely as nominalists continued stubbornly to adhere to one or other form of natural law thinking, even though their philosophical commitments necessitated, with varying degrees of subtlety, forthrightness, and persistence, their shifting away from the version propounded by their metaphysically essentialist (or realist) predecessors, not least among them Aquinas. It is important to be clear on the matter. Contrary to widespread belief, a variety of natural law theories flourished in the Middle Ages. And even if we prescind now from much of that variety, embrace a measure of expository concision, and indulge the type of simplification that teachers instinctively reach for but scholars often regret — even if we do all of that, we must still concede (and, again, widespread belief to the contrary) that the scholastic thinkers of the later Middle Ages passed down to their early modern successors not one but two principal and conflicting traditions of natural law thinking.

II

In this book, then, in which I will be focusing on the ultimate grounding rather than the specific content of natural law theories, I propose to take simply for granted one assumption and to advance three principal arguments.

The assumption, which historians seem less and less disposed to dispute — and that despite the way in which most of us still organize our textbooks and courses of instruction — is that the traditional periodization of European history into ancient, medieval, and modern (an essentially Humanist contrivance) is as much a hindrance as a help when it comes to understanding the course of European intellectual history, that, in effect, it has taken on the appearance of a cumbersomely Ptolemaic system calling for an ever-increasing number of enabling epicycles in order to keep it functioning at all. But while we await with varying degrees of impatience the advent of a definitively Copernican dismantler, life has to go on, and I myself find much to recommend in the claim of historians like Antony Black, Brian Tierney, and J. H. Burns that "the truly epochal shifts in European political thought occurred in the twelfth and eighteenth centuries" and that we would be wise to approach the whole period in between as "essentially a single epoch."[23]

As for my three principal arguments, the first is that much of the variety in natural law thinking across the past two millennia and more, as well as much of the proliferating confusion and ambiguity attendant upon it, reflects the ambiguity of the word *nature* itself and the range of different understandings attaching to it. Years ago, Lovejoy succeeded in teasing apart no less than sixty-six senses in which the word *nature* had been used in antiquity.[24] My own ambitions are a good deal more limited than that. I will be content merely to probe the differences and tensions between what for shorthand purposes may be referred to as the more organismic and more mechanistic usages. I would note further that the variety and confusion in natural law thinking stems also from the differing ways in which theorists have characteristically understood the constitutive moment and obligating force of law — whether, in particular, they have chosen to ground it in indicative rational norm or in imperative legislative command. Finally, I would note that variety and confusion reflects again the differing ways in which theorists have defined the boundaries of the community of being viewed as subject to the sway of natural law. The third-century Roman jurist Ulpian asserted that natural law was "not peculiar to the human race" but is "that which nature has taught all animals."[25] It has been commonplace to bracket that view on the grounds that it admits confusingly into the arena of moral and juridical norms the vastly different scientific notion of "laws" describing observed regularities in the behavior of nonrational entities in the world of physical nature.[26] But, as I mentioned earlier, it is my sense that a certain interpretative price has been paid for too peremptory and thoroughgoing an insistence on that particular conceptual distinction. I stress that here because I believe that we will be in a better position to understand at least one school of early modern juridical natural law thinking if we remain open to the possibility that it may have shared common philosophical or theological roots with the particular notion of scientific laws of nature which rose to prominence in the sixteenth and seventeenth centuries. But the point is worth stressing also — though it is not a topic I will be able to pursue in this book — because contemporary environmental ethicists have become increasingly restive with our traditional drawing of the boundaries of the moral community in such a way as to limit it to human beings alone. As a result, they have attempted to treat animals as rights-bearing agents (thus the utilitarian philosopher Peter Singer) or (as with deep ecologists like Arnie Ness and however elusively argued), to draw still more of the nonhuman world within the perimeter of a less rigidly circumscribed moral community.[27]

My second principal argument will be that, so far, at least, as the last thousand years are concerned, the most important break, shift, or discontinuity in the understanding of natural law, though not, interestingly enough, of natural rights, was that which occurred in the fourteenth and fifteenth centuries. That shift involved changes in the understanding of both the nature of nature and of the essence of law, and it was concerned with the very metaphysical grounding of natural law. It ensured that not one but two principal traditions of natural law thinking would be transmitted to the thinkers of early modern Europe. And it is necessary to take into account the continuing dialectical interchange between those two traditions if one is to make adequate sense of what was going on intellectually in the array of natural law theories framed during the sixteenth, seventeenth, and even eighteenth centuries.

Third, and finally, it will be my purpose to argue that what precipitated this particular shift or discontinuity within the orbit of scholastic philosophy and theology was the renewed pressure on modes of thought, Neoplatonic or Aristotelian in origin, of extra-philosophical commitments of biblical provenance, not least among them the alien insistence on the untrammeled freedom, transcendence, and omnipotence of God. The achievement of the church fathers and their medieval scholastic successors in appropriating for their own purposes the philosophic legacy of Hellenic and Hellenistic antiquity and in harmonizing it with religious commitments of biblical inspiration was a truly remarkable achievement historic in its enduring significance. But we should not miss the fact that it was also an achievement, fraught with instability and tension and predicated at times (or so, over the years, I have come to conclude) on overambitious attempts to render compatible the contradictory and harmonious the dissonant.

As a result, if I may evoke an image to which I have become attached, a profound geologic fault must be supposed to run right across and beneath the often conflicted landscape of our Western intellectual tradition. Along that subterranean and long-forgotten fault, periodic bursts of seismic activity are inevitably to be expected: the bumping, the grinding, the subduction, if you will, of those great tectonic plates of disparate Greek and biblical origin which long ago collided to form the unstable continent of our *mentalité*. And the later Middle Ages, I would suggest, can helpfully be understood as a period distinguished, intellectually speaking, by a recrudescence of precisely such seismic activity leading to, among other things, a reconceptualization of the metaphysical grounding of the law of nature in both the moral/juridical order and the order of physical nature.

These are doubtless large claims, and I should concede at the outset, with profuse apologies to the shade of Lawrence Stone, that they will indeed involve me, from time to time, in his much maligned paper-chase of ideas all the way back to Plato and Aristotle. That said, I propose in the remainder of this chapter to set up the conceptual framework within which in subsequent chapters I will be attempting to vindicate those claims.

III

In the stimulating set of philosophical and cosmological lectures he gathered together in 1932 under the general title *Adventures of Ideas,* and teasing apart what he called the "Hellenic and Hellenistic types of mentality," Alfred North Whitehead described the difference between them as roughly "that between speculation and scholarship [or, alternatively, the Learned Tradition]." He also noted that while speculation is fueled by "a deep ultimate faith that through and through the nature of things is penetrable by reason," the "thorough-going scholar... [is apt to resent]...the airy speculation which connects his own patch of knowledge with that of his neighbour." That conceded, he himself nonetheless argued that both speculation and scholarship as well as the ongoing interplay between them are necessary if we are to have progress in knowledge and advancement in understanding. And in so arguing, he was, I believe, quite right. In particular, and leaning it may be into the prevailing intellectual wind, I would hope that, as a discipline, intellectual history or history of ideas will prove in the end to be a big enough tent or, if you will, sufficiently broad-church in its sensibilities to accommodate, along with its properly specific scholarly preoccupations, the type of intuitive insight responding to the internal logic of ideas that Whitehead himself so powerfully evinced in his own illuminating flights of creative speculation. This is true not least of all here, where he produces an intriguing typology of the main doctrines concerning the laws of nature (physical nature) prevalent in his own lifetime. While he himself was concerned with the analysis of cosmological assumptions, two of the doctrines he identifies, as well as the contrast he draws between them, are, I believe, as valid and relevant in the juridical and ethical sphere as in the scientific. I propose, then, to take them as my point of departure.[28]

The crucial contrast Whitehead draws is that between laws of nature perceived as immanent in the very structure of reality itself and laws of nature conceived of as imposed on the universe as it were from without. By the doctrine of law as immanent, he says, "it is meant that the order of nature expresses the characters of the real things which jointly compose the existences to be found in nature." It involves the assumption that a grasp of the nature of those things will disclose the pattern of their mutual relations one with another. Thus "some partial identity of pattern in the various characters of natural things issues in some partial identity of pattern in the mutual relations of those things." The laws of nature are the formulations of these identities of pattern. Thus, Ulpian-fashion, it could be adduced as a law of nature that animals unite to produce offspring. Or, Aristotelian fashion, that stones released in midair strive necessarily to reach the ground or, rather, to reach their proper place at the center of the universe. This view of the law of nature involves, Whitehead concludes, "some plausible metaphysical doctrine according to which the characters of the relevant things in nature are the outcome of their interconnections, and their interconnections are the outcome of their characters." In effect, it involves some metaphysical "doctrine of Internal Relations."[29]

The doctrine of imposed law, on the other hand, "adopts the alternate metaphysical doctrine of External Relations between the singular things which collectively constitute the world of nature." These singular existents are regarded as the ultimate constituents of nature. As such, they are conceived to possess no inherent connections, one with another, but to be comprehensible each in "complete disconnection" from any other. The relationships into which they enter with "the other ultimate constituents of nature" are imposed on them from without by the sovereign law-giver we call God. And what we have become accustomed to calling the laws of nature are, in effect, these imposed behavior patterns. Because of the crucial element of imposition, it follows that this doctrine differs from what Whitehead goes on to identify as a third, distinct, and essentially positivistic doctrine of laws of nature as mere description. It follows, too, that these imposed behavior patterns are not to be discovered by even the most assiduous scrutiny of the characters of the related things. No amount of study, for example, of bodies at rest will tell us anything about their possible motion. Nor, conversely, can the natures of the related things be deduced by analyzing the laws governing their relations.[30]

Whitehead concedes, forthrightly and not without a certain relish, that both of these opposed doctrines lead to what he calls "the dubieties of metaphysics." That is to say, we should not miss the fact that both doctrines are entailed by, or embedded in, or serve as presuppositions for, or even yearn urgently toward, rival metaphysical schemata the broad outlines of which I should like to sketch in. And presupposed in both cases by that exercise is the assumption that in any coherent, and more or less complete philosophical system there are intimate interconnections, dictated either by strict logical entailment or looser intellectual implication or affinity, among the positions a thinker is led to adapt in natural theology, epistemology, natural, moral, and legal philosophy — perhaps also in political philosophy as well.

Although Whitehead's rival doctrines of immanent and imposed laws of nature are not situated quite at opposite ends of the doctrinal spectrum, they are situated well apart and are in obvious tension one with another. Thus the notion of laws of nature as immanent implies an equally immanent understanding of moral or juridical natural law and may be said to presuppose a system of ideas in which the divine is conceived as immanent or innerworldly; the epistemology is essentialist (or to use the medieval term "realist"); and nature is conceived in organismic terms, fraught with purpose and finality and open to investigation by analytic or deductive modes of reasoning capable of delivering knowledge that is certain or absolute. On the other hand, the notion of laws of nature as imposed by an external will implies a similarly legislative notion of moral or juridical natural law, and presupposes or entails a system which harbors a notion of God as extraworldly or transcendent stressing above all his freedom and omnipotence, a nominalist epistemology, and a natural philosophy of empirical mode or mechanistic sympathies focused on the investigation of efficient causes and emphasizing the conditional nature of all knowledge based on observation of a created and radically contingent world which could well have been other than it is.[31]

If I had to risk putting some shreds of historical flesh on these ungrateful speculative bones — and I suppose I do — I would adduce Hellenistic Stoicism as exemplary of the doctrine of law as immanent. For the Stoics conceived of the physical world as an organic unity impregnated with a reason they regarded as divine. Natural law, therefore, they conceived as universally valid and inherent in the very structure of things — so much so, indeed, that they could draw arguments for peace from the harmony of the celestial spheres. Thus, Diogenes Laertius in his life of Zeus attributes to the Stoics the view that

> living virtuously is equivalent to living in accordance with the experience of the actual course of nature;... for our undivided natures are parts of the nature of the whole universe. And this is why the [moral] end may be defined as life in accordance with nature.... [It is] a life in which we refrain from every action forbidden by the law common to all things, that is to say, the right reason which pervades all things and is identical with Zeus, lord and ruler of all that is.[32]

And as exemplar of the second or imposed system I would adduce the seventeenth-century philosopher Thomas Hobbes, taking seriously, as I do, his more theological moments, and sympathizing, therefore, with the types of interpretative approach pursued by such as Michael Oakeshott, Willis Glover, Howard Warrender, and, most recently, A. P. Martinich.[33] For it was Hobbes, as Oakeshott puts it in discussing what he calls the tradition of Will and Artifice, who elaborated a "comprehensive system where before there were only scattered aphorisms." And characteristic of that Hobbesian system, he says, the thought as it were which pervades its parts, is the understanding of the universe as the contingent creation of an omnipotent divine will; the understanding of the "civil order," accordingly, as an artificial creation of a concatenation of individual acts of autonomous human willing; the understanding of philosophical knowledge, accordingly, as "conditional, not absolute," for "there is no effect which the power of [the omnipotent] God cannot produce in many several ways"; the definition of law, divine and natural no less than human, as the mandate of a sovereign will, the effect, that is, of an efficient cause; the understanding of the civil order no less than the world at large "on the analogy of a machine, where to explain an effect we go to its immediate [efficient] cause; and to seek the result of the cause we go to its immediate effect"; and the concomitant banishment from the realm of law and politics no less than from the natural world of those age-old teleological preoccupations which ill-accorded with so mechanistic an understanding of reality.[34]

Finally, because of the influence it was to exert in subsequent centuries, I would take note of the mediating, quasi-immanentist position that Plato hammered out, though nowhere does he speak explicitly of laws of nature.[35] And the Plato in question was not the Plato of the *Republic,* for down to the fifteenth century, because of the accidents of manuscript transmission, Europeans were acquainted with no more than the name and reputation of that great dialogue. Instead, it is the cosmologist Plato of the *Timaeus* — for medievals *the* quintessential Platonic dialogue. This is the Plato who conceived the world as itself a living, divine being possessed of soul, through its participation in the eternally subsistent forms, archetypes, or ideas fraught with an indwelling and immanent rational order; that order, by virtue of the alignment with the macrocosm of the microcosm of the individual soul, being reflected also in the norms of justice with the help of which human beings strive to live moral lives and construct the just societies that make such lives possible. In all of this, the emphasis is on the explanatory principles to which Cicero was later to attach the terms final and formal causes. It is true that in the mysterious figure of the Demiurgos or world-maker whom Plato introduces in the *Timaeus* we do encounter what appears to be a supreme efficient cause. But as a cause he is severely constrained in his world-making by the eternal rational archetypes and pre-existing materials with which, as cosmic craftsman, he has to work. And it may be, or so some of the ancients thought, that Plato introduced this mythic figure simply in order to symbolize in dramatic guise that the world itself and all beings in the world are infused with a rational cosmic order, itself immanent, indwelling, and divine.[36]

IV

I have chosen to sketch in the outlines of the two rival metaphysical schemata presupposed by Whitehead's doctrines of immanent and imposed laws of nature because they mark, I believe, the boundaries of the intellectual territory inhabited by natural law discourse across the past two thousand years and more, with different traditions of natural law thinking situated at different points along the continuum stretching from one to the other, some such traditions combining (as did Plato), and with varying degrees of tension and plausibility, elements drawn from both schemata. Of course, as the exemplifications just given already suggest, if we attempt (as now we must) to move from the Whiteheadian speculative mode, which relies, in effect, on the internal logic of ideas, to his scholarly (and, in our case, specifically historical) mode — a much less tidy proposition — we have to confront at least two serious difficulties.

First, we have to face the fact that not all philosophers or natural law thinkers are systematic in their philosophizing. In their engagement with reality they may focus on only one particular set of issues or mode of entry, whether metaphysical, epistemological, natural philosophical, or ethical. Across the course of time, they may also shift their mode of approach, or change their minds, or focus sequentially on different sets of issues, perhaps even in ways that appear to be mutually incompatible, thus presenting the historical interpreter with the type of challenge particularly well exemplified (and as we shall see) by the writings of the great fourteenth-century philosopher and theologian, William of Ockham.

Second, as we move to the historical mode we have also to face the more general fact that people in the past did their thinking (as, perforce, do we today) not necessarily as, logically speaking, they *should*, or even as in an ideal philosophical world they *would*, but rather (within their own intellectual limits and given the conditions, challenges, complexities, and confusions of their time) they did that thinking simply as they *could*.

Those craven qualifications duly signaled, let me note that in the remaining chapters I propose to focus, first, on the late medieval shaping of the peculiar notion of scientific laws of nature that later rose to prominence in the sixteenth and seventeenth centuries, then on the twin traditions of moral or juridical natural law thinking bequeathed by the late medieval to the early modern world, and, finally, on the currently quite lively debate concerning the origins of the modern notion of natural rights. And my mode of engagement will be, in Whitehead's terms, scholarly/historical rather than speculative.

Two

LAWS OF NATURE
The Scientific Concept

Let me begin with three quotations, the second and third of which might plausibly be presented as some sort of reply to the first were it not for the fact that they long predate it and hail from a vastly different culture at the opposite end of the earth. The first quotation I draw from one of the studies affiliated with the vast series *Science and Civilization in China* begun by the late Joseph Needham, sinologist and biochemist, and still in progress under different authorship. In that study, Needham made much of the apparent absence from the multiple schools of thought prevalent at one time or another in China of the notion of scientific laws of nature. Even after the Jesuit mission introduced that notion to the Chinese, it met, he says, with little response, and by way of illustrating that observation, he cited the following passage written in 1737:

> The Chinese atheists, says a missionary, are not more tractable with relation to Providence than [they are] with regard to [the Christian doctrine of] the Creation. When we teach them that God, who created the universe out of nothing, governs it by general Laws, worthy of his infinite Wisdom, and to which all creatures conform with a wonderful regularity, they say, that these are high-sounding words to which

35

they can affix no idea, and which do not at all enlighten their understanding. As far as what we call laws, answer they, we comprehend an Order established by a Legislator, who has the power to enjoin them, to creatures capable of executing these laws, and consequently capable of knowing and understanding them. If you say that God has established Laws, to be executed by Beings capable of knowing them, it follows that animals, plants, and in general all bodies which act conformable to those Universal Laws, have a knowledge of them, and consequently that they are endowed with understanding, which [they say] is absurd.[1]

The second quotation I draw from Robert Boyle (Boyle of Boyle's Law) traditionally referred to (rather optimistically, it may be) as the founder of modern chemistry and (less disputably) as "the great father figure of British natural philosophy" in the late-seventeenth century.[2] The word *law*, he conceded, can be applied only in a figurative sense to the behavior of irrational entities, so that "the actions of inanimate bodies, which cannot incite or moderate their own actions, are produced by real power, not by laws." For law is "a moral, not a physical cause." And he added that though "for brevity's sake" he himself, like others, did not scruple to speak of "the laws of nature" which depended "upon the will of the divine author of things," it remained true that law, strictly speaking, is "but a notional thing, according to which, an intelligent and free agent is bound to regulate its actions," such agents alone being able to "regulate the exertions of their power by settled rules."[3]

And the third quotation, drawn from Francisco Suarez, the great Spanish legal philosopher who wrote earlier on in the seventeenth century, could easily be presented, though again anachronistically so, as an endorsement of Boyle's position but with the addition of one very important refinement. Having spoken of God's operating "in accordance with the common laws which he has established in the universe," he too, in relation to the world of physical nature, hastened to concede that "things lacking reason are, properly speaking, capable neither of law nor of obedience." Nonetheless, he added, the legal metaphor still holds in that those "common laws [of nature] ... established in the universe" ultimately reflect a divine mode of operation. They reflect, that is to say, God's action in accordance with "the ordinary law which he has imposed *upon himself.*"[4]

These are intrinsically interesting statements, but if I adduce them now it is less because of that than because they throw a certain light on what is distinctive about the particular notion of laws of nature that rose to such prominence in the sixteenth and seventeenth centuries as a crucial feature of the new departures then occurring in the physical sciences and of the new philosophies of nature that undergirded them. I noted in my first chapter that it has become a commonplace for commentators on natural law theory to bracket as conceptually distinct from the essentially prescriptive moral and juridical usage the scientific notion of laws describing observed regularities in the behavior of entities in the world of physical nature. In that vein, Needham himself acknowledges that "in the outlook of modern science there is, or course, no residue of the notion of command and duty in the 'Laws of Nature.' They are now thought of [rather] as statistical regularities, valid only in given times and places, descriptions not prescriptions." But for him, thinking, as he was, cross-culturally, the question remained as to "whether the recognition of such statistical regularities and their mathematical expression could have been reached by any ... road [other] than that which Western sciences actually travelled."[5] And that road involved passage through a phase during the crucial early modern stage of what used to be called simply "the Scientific Revolution,"[6] when the regnant notion of laws of nature, not yet of course conceived statistically, was also not merely descriptive but, beyond that, in some measure prescriptive. Let me try to explain what I could possibly mean by that.

I

Harking back to my first chapter, let me say that what was involved was, in effect, a phase during which what Whitehead calls the doctrine of imposed law dominated and, with it, the affiliated view of nature which R. G. Collingwood well characterized by contrasting it with the view dominant among the thinkers of Greek antiquity. And that basic contrast he saw as springing from the difference between their respective analogical approaches to nature.

Whereas, he argued, the Greek view of nature as an intelligent organism "saturated or permeated by mind" was based on an analogy between macrocosm and microcosm, between the world of nature and the individual human being, the early modern view — or, more properly, that early modern view which made possible the development of the classical or Newtonian physical science — conceived the world analogically as a machine. Instead of being regarded as capable of ordering its own movements in a rational manner and according to its immanent laws, the world, in such a view, is devoid both of intelligence and life, the movements which it exhibits are imposed on it from without, and "their regularity...due to 'laws of nature' likewise imposed from without." Collingwood concluded, therefore, that this view presupposed both "the human experience of designing and constructing machines and the Christian idea of a creative and omnipotent God."[7]

This is, I believe, a helpful way of characterizing the change in philosophical outlook which made possible the development of the classical or Newtonian physical science. It is, no doubt, an historical commonplace that this change in approach entailed the rejection of the Aristotelian physics, with its apparatus of final causes and ultimate explanations of natural processes, and its replacement with a more empirical natural science preoccupied with quantity, efficient causality, conditional or probable explanations, and power over nature. But Collingwood does well to remind us of the intimate relationship between this change in approach and the rise to prominence of the concept of imposed laws of nature.

In probing this particular phenomenon, it was Needham's hope, by an ambitious exercise in a species of cross-cultural analysis and counterfactual argumentation, to throw some light on the failure of a civilizational tradition as rich and highly sophisticated, intellectually speaking, as the Chinese to engineer the type of critical scientific breakthrough that occurred in early modern Europe. My own purpose here is a much more modest one: simply to try to explain why it was that from the long-enduring tradition of discourse surrounding ancient and medieval notions of natural law there emerged in the early modern period the particular tradition of thinking about physical laws of nature on which Needham chose to focus. Just as discourse about the moral and juridical notion of natural law had embraced a variety of different theories on the matter, so, too, the affiliated and often overlapping tradition of discourse about laws of nature. For however loose-limbed and intermittent it was, we now know that what amounted to such a tradition of discourse did indeed exist.[8]

Prevalent among the Stoics — and the famous statement of the jurist Ulpian constitutes a responsive echo — was the notion that there was a natural law, at once both prescriptive and descriptive, governing not only the moral behavior of human beings but also the very order of the cosmos itself. During Roman antiquity and the medieval centuries, moreover, one finds the term *law* (*lex*) — often used interchangeably with *rule* (*regula*) — employed to denote the principles of such disciplines as mathematics and logic[9] and extended, at least intermittently, to describe regularities in the behavior of phenomena in the physical world. If, by the thirteenth century, this last usage had faded away among those writing on nature, there is one very important exception to that generalization. It is none other, in fact, than that extraordinary figure, the thirteenth-century Franciscan scholastic Roger Bacon, on whose remarkably "modern" use of *law* in his optics Alistair Crombie may have been the first to comment some forty years ago now, and this not without reason, for Bacon referred repeatedly not only to the "law(s) of refraction" but also to "the common laws of nature."[10] So struck, indeed, was Crombie by Bacon's usage that he saw it as part of a "programme for mathematicizing physics" and shifting "the object of scientific inquiry from the Aristotelian 'nature' or 'form' to laws of nature in a recognizably modern sense."[11]

If Needham took serious note of that claim he still, in effect, brushed it to one side on the grounds that Bacon's notion "simply did not win general acceptance in his day."[12] And if an attempt has subsequently been made to demonstrate that it left a bit more of a legacy than Needham supposed, the lines of transmission adduced still remain somewhat tenuous and indirect.[13] Even were that not the case, moreover, the fact remains that to the notion of laws of nature embedded in Bacon's optics attach no theological or prescriptive connotations.[14] And yet from Descartes onwards the idea of divine legislation constituted an integral aspect of the particular concept of laws of nature that played so central a role in the new physical science and affiliated philosophies of nature vigorously promoted by such natural philosophers as Pierre

Gassendi, Walter Charleton, Robert Boyle, and others all the way down to Newton himself, and that set the pace for the great scientific advances of the era. So central, indeed, was this notion for Descartes himself that he portrayed God, on the analogy of a mighty earthly king, as the omnipotent legislator and, as such, the efficient cause of the laws he imposed on nature — not merely, that is, the laws of motion and inertia upon which the mechanistic physics rested, but, more startlingly, the laws of mathematics and logic. For of those eternal truths within which the laws of nature are embedded God is also the author, so much so (though the very thought defies our merely human comprehension) that he was free so to act from all eternity that not all the lines from the center of a circle to its circumference would be equal or that twice four would not make eight.[15]

Those among the natural philosophers of novel leanings who came after Descartes did not go quite that far. Had they done so, indeed, the natural philosophies they developed would have been vastly different than they were. As John Locke was later to put it, it was precisely because the laws governing matter or motion and possessing a "constant and regular connexion in the ordinary course of Things" *lacked* the absolute necessity pertaining to mathematical propositions that they had to be attributed "to nothing else but the arbitrary Determination [or arbitrary Will and good Pleasure] of that All-wise Agent, who has made them to be, and to operate as they do, in a way wholly above our weak Understanding to conceive."[16] Hence the insistence of the scientists that "the laws of motion, without which the present state and course of things could not be maintained" are dependent "upon the will of the divine author of things" (thus Boyle).[17] Or that "the business of true philosophy is ... to inquire after those laws on which the Great Creator actually chose to found this most beautiful Frame of the World, not those by which he might have done the same, had he so pleased" (thus Roger Cotes in his Preface to the second edition of Newton's *Mathematical Principles of Natural Philosophy*). Or that God is the Being who "governs all things, not as the soul of the world, but as Lord over all," by his own will imposing laws of nature upon the celestial bodies, "cooperating with all things according to accurate laws . . . except where it is good to act otherwise" (thus Newton himself).[18]

And perhaps we should add that in his own preface to the first edition of the *Mathematical Principles* Newton also tells us that the modern investigators of nature, "rejecting [the] substantial forms and occult qualities [of the ancients], have endeavored to subject the phenomena of nature to the laws of mathematics." There could be no question of these laws being intrinsic to the natures of things. No amount of study of bodies at rest will tell us anything about their possible motion, for motion is not the outcome of some hidden potentiality, but simply the effect of "forces impressed." And such forces, as he adds in the *Opticks*, could well be different than they are, for God could "*vary the laws of nature*, and make worlds of several sorts in several parts of the universe."[19]

The problem outstanding, then, is not why the notion of laws of nature made its appearance in the new scientific thinking of the sixteenth and seventeenth centuries. There was, after all, nothing altogether novel about that notion *as such*. The real question is why this particular understanding or this particular tradition of thought within the broader and quite varied tradition of discourse concerning laws of nature rose to a position of such prominence in the early modern philosophies of nature. As Edgar Zilsel insisted in 1942 (and he was, I believe, the first to focus on the question), it cannot be regarded as identical with the whole vast problem of explaining the rise of the modern experimental science. It did not follow that when the scientific *virtuosi* came to focus on the effort to detect in nature mechanical regularities susceptible of mathematical formulation they should also have interpreted them as *divinely imposed* laws. The fact that they did so interpret them had to be the outcome, in his opinion, of concomitant political and social developments. Starting out, then, with the general assumption that the idea of a reign of God over the world must have resulted from "a comparison of nature and state," from a transfer into the divine realm of men's conceptions of earthly kings and their reigns, he moved on to the related historical assumption that the Stoic doctrine of a universal natural law was to be correlated with the rise of great monarchies in the Hellenistic era after Alexander the Great. Those assumptions duly made, it seemed equally reasonable to him to relate the rise of the concept of physical laws of nature in the sixteenth and seventeenth centuries to the decline of feudalism, the beginnings of capitalism, and the reappearance of royal absolutism. "[I]t is no mere chance," he said, "that the Cartesian idea of God as the legislator of the universe developed only forty years after Jean Bodin's theory of sovereignty."[20]

That Needham should later have concurred in this explanation — it "must surely be in principle," he said, "the right one"[21] — is really quite odd, fraught as it is with multiple difficulties. Not the least of those difficulties, as he himself admits, is that it "brings us face to face with the paradox that in China, where imperial absolutism covered a longer period" than in the West, we hardly meet at all with the idea of laws of nature, certainly not the idea in question of divinely imposed laws.[22] But even if one brackets that particular concern, it should be noted that Zilsel's explanation is predicated on a failure to recognize the crucial distinction that Whitehead detected between laws of nature conceived as immanent in the very structure of the world and springing from the very natures of the beings that compose that world, and such laws conceived in the manner characteristic of the seventeenth-century scientific *virtuosi* as behavior patterns imposed on the world from without and reflecting the mandates of an omnipotent creator God. Once this distinction is made, Zilsel's ascription of the rise of Stoic ideas of laws of nature (quintessentially immanentist after all) to the pervasive influence of growing royal absolution ceases to be obvious.

Descartes, it is true, in advancing the idea of divinely imposed laws of nature had indeed invoked the analogy of the legislator king, but it should be realized that there was nothing at all novel about the deployment in argument of such God-king (or, sometimes, God-pope) parallelisms. They constitute, in fact, something of a cliché in the theological, philosophical, and juristic literature from at least the late thirteenth century on at least to the early eighteenth, at which point they put in an appearance in the physico-theological arguments embedded in the celebrated Clarke-Leibniz correspondence. I would emphasize, moreover, that on this matter the ideological traffic was not unidirectional but reciprocal. That is to say, the parallelism was invoked just as often, by adducing God's mode of action, in an attempt to clarify the reach of the legal and governmental powers of the human sovereign, whether royal, papal, or imperial, as it was in order to elucidate the workings of the divine power by referring to the human analogy. This was quintessentially so in the political writings of that learned monarch James I of England, who was never more eloquent (in a slightly elephantine sort of way) than when invoking and analyzing the divine power in order to elucidate his own kingly prerogatives, and who in so doing elaborated what amounted, in fact, to a royal theology.[23]

But if a royal theology could be a moving force in seventeenth-century political thinking, why should we need to resort to elaborate sociopolitical explanations, at once both cumbersome and imprecise, in order to explain the rise to prominence among the early modern scientific thinkers of the notion of divinely imposed laws of nature? In order to shed some light on what they themselves called the physico-theology of their era, would not one be better advised *a priori* to explore changes in the preceding philosophical tradition and especially the sector of that tradition pertaining to what is normally classified as natural or philosophical theology? That, certainly, is the exploration I propose to undertake. And it is an exploration which will involve me (with renewed apologies to Stone's illustrious shade) in yet another paper-chase of ideas all the way back to the ancients, but at the same time one that will lead me to the conclusion that it is in the fourteenth and fifteenth centuries that one can discern the shift in viewpoint crucial to the later emergence of the new understanding of physical laws of nature.

II

There can be few developments in the history of philosophy more tangled and more complex than the movement of ideas in late antiquity that culminated in the fourth century of the Christian era in the Neoplatonic patterns of thought which St. Augustine encountered in what he was wont to call "the books of the Platonists."[24] Among other things, this movement had involved a persistent tendency to understand the mysterious Demiurgos of Plato's *Timaeus* not as a mythic symbol but as a real, creative efficient cause of the world, to conflate him, nonetheless, with the transcendent and uncaring Unmoved Mover of Aristotle's *Metaphysics,* the Final and highest Good which he himself calls "god," — and, in a crucially influential move, to treat Plato's eternally subsistent forms, archetypes, or ideas, not as independently and eternally subsistent entities, but as thoughts or ideas in the mind of the supreme God resulting from that cosmic conflation. Thus emerged the notion of a transcendent God, at once the highest good or final cause to which all things lovingly aspire (as Dante was later, and accurately, to put it: *"l'amor que muove il sole e l'altre stelle"*), the first efficient cause to which all things owe their existence, the supreme reason (or formal cause) from which all things derive their order and intelligibility, and increasingly (for Neoplatonism was no less a path of salvation than a philosophy) the object of a lively devotional sentiment.

Given this development, it is not too hard to understand how St. Augustine, following the trail blazed in Alexandria by Philo Judaeus in the first century of the Christian era and later broadened by the Greek church fathers, was able, in a triumphant achievement of philosophico-theological bridge-building and in a fashion that proved to be definitive for Western Christian philosophy, to engineer a further and quite stunning conflation. It was nothing other, in effect, than the conflation of the Neoplatonic God—the God of the philosophers, as it were, in its final, most complex, and most developed form — with the biblical God of Abraham, Isaac, and Jacob, the personal God of power and might who not only transcends the universe but also created it, not out of Platonic or Aristotelian pre-existent matter but out of nothing, the providential God, moreover, from whose omniscient purview not even the fall of a sparrow escapes and against whose miraculous intervention not even the might of a Nebuchadnezzar was proof. In so doing, Augustine attempted to close the way to any further Christian flirtation with the Greek notion of the eternity of the world such as that indulged in by the Alexandrian theologian Origen two centuries earlier. At the same time, by agreeing with Philo, the Neoplatonists, and many of his Christian predecessors that the creative act was indeed an intelligent one guided by forms, archetypes, or ideas of the Platonic mold, but ideas now situated in the divine mind itself as a sort of creative blueprint, he responded to the Greek concern to vindicate philosophically the order and intelligibility of the universe. By virtue of his authority, then, he secured for the doctrine of the divine ideas an enduring place in later Christian philosophy. Clearly, an extraordinary accommodation.

That duly acknowledged, I must now insist that what it reflected was a victory for delicate philosophical and theological diplomacy rather than the achievement of any truly stable synthesis. The doctrine of the divine ideas itself witnesses to the severe internal tensions that Augustine's attempted synthesis involved. In the historic encounter between the Greek philosophical tradition and religious views of biblical provenance, the great stumbling block had been (and was to remain) the sheer difficulty of reconciling the personal and transcendent biblical God of power and might, upon whose will the very existence of the universe was radically contingent, with the characteristically Greek intuition of the divine as limited and innerworldly and of the universe as necessary and eternal — or, to put it somewhat differently, with the persistent tendency of the Greek philosophers to identify the divine with the immanent and necessary order of an eternal cosmos.[25] The retention of the Platonic ideas reflects the impact of that enduring tension. The denial of their independent existence and their location in the mind of God, on the other hand, reflects the desire to make room for the biblical conception of the divine as almighty power and unimpeded will. But the nagging question of course remained: Was it room enough? If the universe was truly rational and ultimately intelligible, could God ever be willful? And if God could really be willful, could the universe be fully rational and intelligible? What had guaranteed the bedrock rationality of Plato's universe, after all, had been the subordination of the Demiurge's craftsman-like creative activity to the patterns, blueprints, or archetypes presented to him in the independent and co-eternal forms or ideas. But when the biblical Job had sought some justification, comprehensible in human terms, for the disasters his Hebraic God had visited upon him, God's only reply (as Hobbes did not fail to note) was not a reassuring vindication of the rationality and stability of his justice, but rather a disdainful and terrifying evocation of his omnipotence. "Where were you when I laid the foundation of the earth?...Have you commanded the morning since your days began?...Can you bind the chains of the Pleiades, or loose the cords of Orion?...Shall a faultfinder contend with the Almighty?"[26]

The tensions, then, were present already in Augustine, and they were to mount in intensity during the course of the twelfth and thirteenth centuries with the progressive recovery of the entire corpus of Aristotelian writings and its prior communication in Arabic form, confusingly interwoven with the paraphrases and commentaries of the Muslim philosophers Ibn Sina and Ibn Rushd, or Avicenna and Averroës as they came to be known in the world of Latin Christendom. Thus the somewhat occluded Aristotle with whom the scholastics had first to cope, and the Aristotle whom the ecclesiastical authorities at Paris at first moved nervously to condemn, was one who appeared to teach not only the eternity of the world but also its necessity. His world, that is to say, was not a *created* world presupposing the free decision of a divine will, but a world that eternally and necessarily flowed from the divine principle on the analogy of a stream flowing from its source or of a logical conclusion proceeding necessarily from its premise. As such, it was a determined world in which everything had to be what it was and in which there was room neither for the providence of God nor the free will of man. Nor did the eventually successful effort to penetrate the veil of commentary and to isolate the authentic teaching of Aristotle himself make the successful reconciliation of his views with Christian belief by any means a trouble-free enterprise, as Robert Boyle himself was later to point out.[27] For by Boyle's time in the latter years of the seventeenth century it had become clear that not even the subtle philosophical and theological diplomacy of an Aquinas had proved capable of convincing the more conservative of his contemporaries and the more cautious among his scholastic successors that the particular accommodation he himself had proposed was truly viable without the modification of beliefs so fundamental to Christianity as to be nonnegotiable.

What had ensued in the late thirteenth, fourteenth, and fifteenth centuries was, as a result, a set of philosophical and theological developments of formidable complexity, the interpretation of which has in many ways been transformed over the course of the past half century but which remains fraught with scholarly disagreements of the most technical and sophisticated kind, and which, in the brief compass of this chapter, I cannot aspire to decode with even a remotely adequate degree of specificity and nuance. Let me simply push through to the heart of the matter, at least as I intuit it. And for me, coming to it, as I do, with Plato's *Timaeus* and Philo's commentary on Genesis in mind, the Neoplatonic and Augustinian doctrine of the divine ideas must occupy center stage.

What Aquinas in fact did was to edge beyond the hallowed "negative way" of attempting to come to terms with the divine nature in accordance with which, rather than aspiring to know what God is, we must content ourselves with groping our way through the darkness of being in an attempt to identify what God is *not*. Instead, he argued that by extrapolating from our human knowledge of created things and by recourse to an analogical use of terms, it was possible without equivocation to predicate of God such positive attributes as intelligence, wisdom, and goodness.

Bolder in his rationalism than many of his more cautious contemporaries, he set out by blending Aristotelian and Augustinian notions (including the doctrine of the divine ideas) to demonstrate that God's creative act was not only a free but also — and, in humanly comprehensible terms — a rational one, thus vindicating the order, rationality, and intelligibility of the universe.

Assuming the primacy of reason over will, not only in man but also in God, he regarded what in later parlance would be called the physical laws of nature, and also the moral and juridical natural law, in comparatively "Greek" fashion as, both of them, the external manifestation of an indwelling and immanent reason. Thus, law in general being for him "something pertaining to reason," he viewed the divine "reason," which directs "the government of things" and exists "in God as ruler of the universe," as itself possessing "the nature of 'law' in which all beings, in some manner, participate ... [deriving] ... from it certain inclinations to those actions and aims which are proper to them." That "eternal law," then, orders to their appropriate ends all created beings, irrational "as well as rational, and it is to be understood as "nothing other than the idea of the divine wisdom insofar as it directs all acts and movements" and governs "the whole community of the universe."[28]

It was the advantage of this way of looking at things that it enabled one to regard the whole of being, the realm of nature no less than that of man, as in some fashion subject to the norms of the same eternal law. The correlative disadvantage, however, was that that subjection to law could equally be taken to extend to God himself, thus threatening at worst to turn him into a merely demiurgic figure limited in his creative activity by the co-eternal forms, archetypes, or ideas, or at best casting a dangerously qualifying shadow athwart his freedom and omnipotence. For the eternal law is nothing other than one aspect of the divine reason itself, and in God reason is prior to will. It would appear, then, that the old discord between disparate Greek and biblical notions of the divine, far from being resolved in the ingenious accommodations sponsored by the theology of the schools, was simply transposed into another key, sounding now, as it were, in the celestial harmonics of the divine psychology itself and threatening, at least in the view of the more cautious of contemporary theological diagnosticians, the onset even of a species of divine schizophrenia. For some, in effect, the tensions involved in Aquinas's doctrine of eternal law and in all that it both presupposed and entailed had not merely survived but had been dangerously intensified.

Of the shift in mood that ensued among the theologians of Paris and Oxford, the condemnation as contrary to the Christian faith of a host of philosophical propositions (including some attributable to Aquinas) which Étienne Tempier, archbishop of Paris, issued in 1277 on the advice of a theological commission were as much symptom as cause. During the century following his death in 1274, then, many of the rationalistic convictions characteristic of Aquinas and of those so-called realists who either trod in his footsteps or in some measure shared in his fundamental essentialism were called into question, especially so by the somewhat varied group of thinkers who pursued what came to be known as "the modern way," who came to be labeled as nominalists, and who were seen to have drawn their inspiration, at one or other remove, from the philosophical and theological writings of the great fourteenth-century English philosopher and theologian William of Ockham.[29] Prominent among them during the fourteenth and fifteenth centuries were such thinkers as Robert Holcot, Adam Wodeham, Pierre d'Ailly, and Gabriel Biel. None of them, I realize, are exactly household names today, though in intellectual stature they arguably bear comparison with such better known early modern figures as Mersenne, Malebranche, Boyle,

Pascal, and Berkeley. Nor were they thinkers of identical commitments. But they can all be said to have distanced themselves from the priority accorded to the divine intellect over the divine will and from the confidence shared by Aquinas in the capacity of analogical reasoning to cast a conceptual net really capable of encompassing in a meaningful commonality of discourse the natures of both God and man and bridging the gulf dividing the finite from the infinite.

This last appears to have been one of the fundamental issues at stake in the late medieval and early modern dispute about whether in God reason is prior to will or vice versa. All of these thinkers were careful, of course, to insist with Ockham that "there is no distinction [i.e., lack of identity] between the will and essence and will and intellect" of God.[30] But they all go on nevertheless, if behind a screen of caveats, to draw precisely such a distinction. To say, says Pierre d'Ailly, that we can distinguish by reason between the divine will and intellect can be regarded, though not literally true, as the abbreviated expression of something that is true and corresponds, after all, with "the way of speaking of the saints and the learned." For "these terms [will and intellect], standing for the same thing, have diverse and distinct ideas corresponding to them in the [human] mind."[31]

Hence the growing inclination in the fourteenth century among those of nominalist commitment, taking the omnipotence of God as their fundamental principle, to accord to the divine will the primacy in God's workings *ad extra,* that is to say, not in himself but in relation to his creatures. With that went a concomitant understanding of the order of the created world (both the natural order governing the behavior of nonrational beings and, as we shall see, the moral order governing human behavior) no longer as a participation in a divine reason that is in some measure transparent to the human intellect, but rather as the deliverance of a free and inscrutable divine will. And this divine will is bound by no external standard and is utterly resistant to the curious probings of any merely human intellect.[32] The hallowed doctrine of the divine ideas came now under challenge and with it the epistemological realism and whole metaphysic of essences in which it was embedded. Also called into question was the affiliated understanding of the universe as an intelligible organism penetrable *a priori* by reason because it was itself ordered and sustained by a luminous, indwelling, and immanent reason. The tendency, therefore, was to set God over against the world he had created and which was constantly dependent upon him; to view it now as an aggregation of particular entities linked solely by external relations, comprehensible (and, if God so chose, capable of existing) each in isolation from the others, and, as a result, open to investigation only by some form of empirical endeavor. The tendency, in effect, harking back to my first chapter, was to move in the direction of the metaphysical schema we saw to be associated with Whitehead's doctrine of imposed laws of nature.

Tendency of course is something of a weasel-word but I use it deliberately and for two reasons. First and in general, I cannot help being conscious of the variations and complexities involved in the pertinent group of scholastic thinkers whom I have in mind, as well as the sheer difficulty scholars have experienced over the past half century and more in their effort to map, correct, and remap the pattern of oppositions, novel departures, disagreements, and affiliations prevalent among them. Second, and more particularly, is the heightened emphasis both in ecclesiastical condemnation and philosophical affirmation on the centrality of the doctrine of divine omnipotence and the concomitant insistence that the physical world is contingent on the divine will no less for its nature and mode of operation than for its very existence. Such things might lead one to expect "medieval natural philosophers to have recognized that the behavior of a contingent world cannot be inferred with certainty from any known set of first principles and, therefore, to have set out to develop empirical methodologies" and to commit themselves to a natural science clearly dependent on observation and experiment.[33] But this, of course, despite shifts in theory, they did not quite succeed in doing for centuries to come. Despite criticism and questioning on this or that point of detail, "natural philosophers and theologians," one historian of science has bluntly insisted, "continued to believe that both the [physical] world and the proper method for exploring it were more or less as Aristotle had described them."[34]

Fair enough, but that "more or less" represents, of course, an important and helpful qualification. For what, willy-nilly, they did was in effect and in a fashion more radical than Aquinas to encapsulate Aristotle's vision of the world within a larger (and ultimately incompatible) religious framework which stripped from that world its eternity and necessity. As a result, they were led also to provincialize the Aristotelian natural philosophy in such a way as ultimately to preclude its claim to be able to deliver via chains of demonstrative syllogistic reasoning a knowledge that was certain. They did so for theological reasons, conscious of the possibility that God could have fashioned vastly different worlds. Accordingly, they confined the Aristotelian prescriptions to the particular world God had actually willed to create, and treated them, therefore, as valid only *ex suppositione* or *ex hypothesi*, for they presuppose the existence of the present dispensation of things, and, even then, rejected them outright when they appeared to impose profane limits on the reach of the divine power, as, for example, did Aristotle's claim that the existence of a vacuum is impossible, or his insistence that the world is eternal. With reference to that latter claim, indeed, Edward Grant has said that it "was to the relations between science and religion in the Middle

Ages what the Copernican heliocentric theory was in the sixteenth and seventeenth centuries and the Darwinian theory of evolution in the nineteenth and twentieth centuries."[35]

In their efforts to cope with such challenges the theologians and natural philosophers of the fourteenth and fifteenth centuries characteristically turned to an already well-established scholastic distinction concerning the power of God. In accordance with that distinction they discriminated between God's power taken as absolute and as ordained (*potentia dei absoluta et ordinata*), using the term "absolute power" to denote God's power taken in itself, that is, his capacity taken *in abstracto* and without reference to the orders of grace, morality, and nature which, of his ordained power, he has actually willed to establish. That distinction they were to pass on, in turn, to the theologians, philosophers, and natural scientists of the sixteenth and seventeenth centuries, and we now know it to have enjoyed a half-millennial currency from the early thirteenth century down at least as far as the early eighteenth. And it lent itself to yeoman-service on the natural-philosophical front, in particular because its impact was such as to preclude the necessity and underline the contingency of the entire divinely established order of nature, while at the same time affirming its *de facto* stability. That impact was two-fold because the distinction inserted side by side with the Old Testament vision of Yahweh as a God of might and power another fundamentally biblical theme, that of God's promise and covenant. The only force capable of binding omnipotence without thereby denying it was, after all, omnipotence itself. While an all-powerful God cannot be bound by the canons of any merely human reason or justice, he is certainly capable by his own free decision of binding himself to follow a certain pattern in dealing with his creation, a pattern dictated by "the ordinary law," which, you will recall, Suarez had

spoken of as God having imposed "upon himself." So the biblical God who knows, of course, no absolute necessity, has freely
chosen to bind himself by what was called a conditional or hypothetical necessity, a "necessity appropriate to God," as Robert
Holcot put it, "because of his promise, that is, his covenant or established law,"[36] just as, to use the somewhat problematic analogy
that became a commonplace in both medieval and early modern
discussions of the matter, an absolute monarch can bind himself
in his dealings with his subjects.[37]

That problematic analogy seems to have appeared so obvious to
people at the time that it entered theological discourse before the
thirteenth century was out and, when it did so, may have encour-
aged the development of a bifurcation in the meanings attached
to the distinction. At its inception, and certainly in the classical
usage favored by Aquinas and many others in the Middle Ages,
the absolute power was not understood as a presently active one
by means of which God intervenes in the world to act apart from
(or set aside) the order he has established by what was called his
ordained power. Instead, it was taken to refer to God's *hypothetical* ability to do many things he does not in fact choose to do.
It denoted God's power in itself, his capacity taken *in abstracto*
and without reference to the orders of grace, morality, and nature he has actually, of his ordained power, willed to establish.[38]
Well before the end of the thirteenth century, however, stimulated it may have been by the resort to monarchical and juridical
analogies, a different understanding of the absolute power had established itself, one that side by side with the classical usage was
in subsequent centuries to endure. It envisaged the possibility that
God's absolute power, by virtue of which he can do anything that
does not involve a formal contradiction, is a potentially active or
operational power whereby he can contravene (and in the course

of history has actually contravened) the laws — natural, salvational, moral — which, by his ordained power, he has actually willed to establish. In accordance with this view miracles can be understood as instances of God's actual exercise of his absolute power. And the example classically invoked — from Pierre d'Ailly in the fourteenth century to Robert Boyle in the seventeenth — is God's intervention to suspend the natural causality of the flames in Nebuchadnezzar's fiery furnace in order to deliver unscathed Shadrach, Meshach, and Abednego.[39]

In recent years it has been demonstrated that not only this power distinction itself but also both ways of understanding the absolute power endured down to the early eighteenth century, and not merely in the writings of such scholastic figures as Ockham, Holcot, d'Ailly, or Andreas de Novocastro in the fourteenth and fifteenth centuries, or John Major, Jacques Almain, Francisco Suarez, and the so-called "Conimbricenses" (or Jesuit commentators on Aristotle at the University of Coimbra) in the sixteenth and seventeenth centuries. Whatever the hesitations or qualifications introduced by Luther and Calvin when they themselves alluded to the distinction, such Lutheran and Calvinist scholastic thinkers as Johann Gerhard, Johann Quenstedt, Francis Turretino, Amandus Polanus, and Johann Alsted managed, nonetheless, to invoke it, and in quite traditional fashion.[40] So, too, in the same period, did such people as Hobbes's distinguished adversary, the Anglican bishop John Bramhall, the so-called "federal" theologians of Old and New England, from William Perkins and William Ames to Increase Mather and Samuel Willard, as well as such natural philosophers and scientific *virtuosi* as Descartes, Mersenne, Gassendi, Walter Charleton, and Robert Boyle. And more than one historian of early modern science has now been led to suggest that "the theological framework of *potentia dei absoluta et ordinata* guided Newton and his contemporaries when they enquired into the relationship between God and the world."[41]

If these early modern natural philosophers and scientists found it helpful to make use of the power distinction that had played so significant a role in the thinking of the late medieval philosophers and theologians, let me suggest that they did so precisely because they shared with those thinkers a marked preoccupation with the omnipotence of God. And they shared with them also a concomitant concern to banish from the world which God had created and which was the object of their probing investigations any lingering traces of the necessity or determinism that was part and parcel of the Aristotelian natural philosophy as the medievals had first received it from the Arab commentators. Thus Descartes insisted that to say that the laws of nature or even the axioms of mathematics were independent of God's will as "supreme legislator" would be to turn him into a mere Jupiter or Saturn and to subject him to the control of the Fates.[42] Thus Pierre Gassendi, insisting that "the thrice great God is not, as [the] Jupiter of the poets is to the fates, bound by things created by him," emphasized the utter contingency of "the course of nature" and the fact that God "is free from the laws of nature which he created by his own free will," and went on to declare that by "virtue of his absolute power he [can] destroy anything he has created."[43] Thus Walter Charleton, who embraced with enthusiasm Gassendi's version of the atomistic mechanical philosophy and was largely responsible for introducing it into England — thus Charleton was also and quite self-consciously aware of the importance of the scholastic heritage, insistent on the overriding omnipotence of God, and careful (in medieval fashion) to affirm the attendant possibility that God, whose power knows no limits, could have created, had he so wished, a plurality of worlds. "[W]e must cautiously abandon," he said, [that more specious opinion of the *Platonist* and *Stoick*] . . . in this, that it . . . blasphemously invades the cardinal Prerogative of Divinity, *Omnipotence,* by denying him [i.e. God] a reserved power of infringing, or altering any one of those [*ordinary* and *establish't* Laws of Nature] which [he] Himself ordained, and enacted, and chaining up his armes in the adamantine fetters of Destiny.[44]

Thus Roger Cotes, writing the preface to the second edition of Newton's *Mathematical Principles,* is careful to state that "the business of true philosophy is . . . to inquire after those laws on which the Great Creator actually chose to found this most beautiful Frame of the World, not those by which he might have done the same had he pleased." From "the perfectly free Will of God directing and presiding over all [have flowed] those . . . laws which we call the laws of Nature . . . , in which there appear many traces indeed of the most wise contrivance, but not the least shadow of necessity."[45] Thus, again, and finally, Robert Boyle, who took as the very point of departure for his natural philosophy and physico-theology the utter freedom and almighty power of God, and recognized the law of noncontradiction and a choice on God's part to oblige himself by promise, covenant, and pact as the only limits on omnipotence, argued, accordingly, that had God so wished, he could have created a better world than he did. Explicitly excoriating the Aristotelian denial to God of both the creation and providential governance of the world, Boyle went on to insist that the laws of nature in general were the product of free, divine volition. God had imposed those laws "arbitrarily" on the brute matter he had himself created, and, if he so chose, or if he so chooses, could or can, as "supreme and absolute God" and by an exercise of his "irresistible, absolute, or supernatural power," contravene those laws, as we know from the Bible he has on occasion actually chosen to do.[46]

In so arguing, it must be insisted, such early modern scientific thinkers were following in the footsteps of many a late medieval theologian and of such late medieval natural philosophers as John Buridan and Marsilius of Inghen, men who had come to conceive of the natural world no longer as a luminous world fraught with comprehensible purpose by virtue of its own indwelling rationality, or as possessing an order grounded in some sort of participation in the divine reason itself and immanent in the very nature of things. Instead, they had come to see it as a contingent and covenanted order reflecting (Suarez-fashion) "the ordinary law" to which God has freely bound himself in his dealings with the created world. And it was that contingent and covenanted order that the scientific virtuosi understood as being expressed in the laws of nature God has imposed upon that world.

III

At the end, then, of this long paper-chase of ideas in search of a solution, perhaps I would be wise to remind you of the precise nature of the question to which it purports to be an answer. Namely, why should it have come about that from the halting, intermittent, and really quite varied tradition of discourse concerning the physical laws of nature prevailing during the centuries preceding, Whitehead's quite specific doctrine of divinely imposed laws of nature should have risen to such prominence in the early modern period? And by way of answer, it has been my purpose to argue that the evidence points insistently to the theologically driven shift in thinking about such things that had occurred already in the fourteenth and fifteenth centuries and had stimulated a move, admittedly complex, halting, and uneven, in the direction of Whitehead's doctrine of imposed law and of the metaphysical schema in which it was embedded.

While during the later Middle Ages the legal metaphor was not applied to the world of nature with the frequency and clarity that was to become a commonplace in scientific writing by the end of the seventeenth century, it was by no means absent from philosophical discourse. Even William of Ockham, whom I have not found using with a clearly scientific connotation the precise terms "laws of nature" or "natural laws," *does* make use of the legal metaphor to denote the fixed order according to which God of his ordained power acts in relation to his creation. Thus, in common with so many other late medieval thinkers, he speaks of "the ordained law" and uses the expressions "by the common law" or "the laws ordained and instituted by God" as synonyms for "in the present order" or "given the divine order."[47] In the same way, though more explicitly, for he discussed such matters in a more thoroughgoing fashion, Pierre d'Ailly, who constantly draws comparisons between God's will as "the first obligating rule or law in the genus of obligatory law" and "the first efficient cause in the genus of efficient causality," employs among others such revealing phrases as "by the common course of nature," "by the common laws and naturally," "naturally, or by the ordained law," or, speaking even more precisely, by "the natural law which God has ordained in things," or "by the laws of the heavens" or other laws which God has imposed upon the world of nature. And, having spoken of the law which God has ordained in natural things, he goes on in one place, as if to emphasize still further the externally imposed nature of that law, to admit the relevance to the universe of that clock analogy which was to be popularized in the seventeenth century by Robert Boyle and to become a cliché of eighteenth-century natural theology.[48]

None of this, of course, would have been of any help to the eighteenth-century Chinese commentators to whom Needham alludes, for, as he himself said and as others have pointed out, they lacked, at least in their dominant and most enduring intellectual traditions, any clear notion of a personal and transcendent legislating deity.[49] But it does afford a clear illustration of the emergence already in the fourteenth century of the notion of physical laws of nature, at once both prescriptive and descriptive, that was to rise to so prominent and central a position in the thinking of the seventeenth-century scientific *virtuosi*. It remains to be seen, then, whether that particular notion of physical laws of nature provides some sort of template to which the cognate notion of moral or juridical natural law can be seen to conform. If from time to time in my remarks so far, I have casually assumed that to be the case, in what follows I am going to have to prove it. And that, I should signal now, will not turn out to be a trouble-free endeavor.

Three

NATURAL LAW
Disputed Moments of Transition

Among the many pungent declamations punctuating the long history of natural law and natural rights discourse, few have attracted more persistent, more concentrated, and, ultimately, more conflicted attention than the celebrated words lodged in the "Prolegomena" to the classic *De jure belli et pacis* ("On the Law of War and Peace") which the Dutch jurist, Hugo Grotius, published in 1625. So, with that, let me begin.

I

Having identified sociability as one of "the traits characteristic of man," and having defined it as the "impelling desire" for a social life that is "peaceful, and organized according to the measure of his intelligence" via "the direction of a well-tempered judgment" itself responsive "to the law of nature, that is the nature of man" — having said all of that, Grotius went on to throw into the hopper the handful of words that were destined to attract so much attention and to be dismissed by Samuel Pufendorf as "an impious and idiotic theory."[1] "What we have been saying," he said, "would have a degree of validity even if we should concede that which cannot be conceded without the utmost wickedness, [namely] that there is no God, or that the affairs of men are of no concern to him."[2]

Although Grotius went on immediately to insist that the very opposite of that view has been "implanted in us" by reason and unbroken tradition, and confirmed by many proofs "as well as by miracles attested by all ages,"[3] that did not preclude his evocation of the "impious hypothesis" from finding its place in what became something of a standard portrayal of him as the very demiurge of moral and jurisprudential modernity, an heroic figure responsible for breaking the ice after the long, gloomy winter of the Middle Ages and dissipating "those thick Clouds of Darkness in which the World has been so long envelop'd."[4] He was, in effect, the man responsible for nothing less than the invention of a new and systematic "science of morality," the natural law thinker who broke finally with classical and medieval natural law doctrines, setting in their place a new and secularized form of natural law, independent of natural no less than of revealed theology. Or, as in some recent formulations at least, he was the man responsible for representing "the concept of natural law . . . [as] . . . derivative from rights"[5] or, perhaps, substituting for the older notion of natural *law*, the more modern doctrine of natural *rights*.

That general portrait gained currency already in the seventeenth century, and though subjected to challenge by some of Grotius's contemporaries, in one version or another it has proved over the long haul and down, indeed, to the present[6] to be remarkably durable. Centuries later, after all, whole generations of students in the Anglophone world were to encounter it in the successive editions of George Sabine's highly popular *History of Political Theory*. For Sabine, it was Grotius who, in effect, "took the final step of detaching natural law from its entanglement in religious authority." "Nothing," he asserts, "shows more clearly his independence of the system of divine sovereignty implicit in Calvinism" than his insistence that the mandates of natural law would retain their validity even if, by hypothesis, there were no God.[7]

Among commentators, it is true, there appears to be little agreement about the precise nature of the novelty, or "modernity," or break with scholastic thought patterns they so persistently (if somewhat mystifyingly) ascribe to Grotius. For some it has been a matter of the content of his natural law teaching, for others the deductive rationalism of his particular jurisprudential method. Nevertheless, whatever the stance adopted, not even the most skeptical would be disposed to claim that there was nothing at all novel about his achievement.[8] My own purpose, however, is not to address that general question of novelty. Instead, it is simply to insist that no real novelty attaches to the way in which he identified the ultimate grounding of natural law, and to insist also that it is, in fact, his very invocation of the impious hypothesis which makes that lack of novelty perfectly clear. This is true for two reasons.

First, that impious hypothesis was far from being itself some sort of extraordinary novelty. "Counterfactual assertions concerning the existence of God," it has well been said, "are commonplace in antiquity, the middle ages and later."[9] In one variant or another something akin to the impious hypothesis crops up in other thinkers of the early modern era, most notably in Gabriel Vasquez (d. 1604) and Francisco Suarez (d. 1632). And though its precise meaning and significance have to be teased out from the text itself, from Grotius's general teaching on natural law in the *De jure belli et pacis,* and from pertinent statements in other of his works, the most likely roots of the hypothesis are to be found engaged in the soil of late medieval philosophical and theological discourse, where comparable or affiliated statements have been identified in a range of thinkers as different from one another in their intellectual affiliations as Duns Scotus (d. 1308), Gregory of Rimini (d. 1358), and Gabriel Biel (d. 1495).[10]

Second, understood in the broader context of his natural law thinking, Grotius's impious hypothesis can be seen to witness less to any great secular novelty than to the continuing dialectic between two distinct theories concerning the metaphysical grounding of natural law which the early modern natural law thinkers had inherited from their medieval and late medieval predecessors. In the *De jure belli et pacis*, it turns out, he was maneuvering for position in such a way as to distance himself from the more voluntaristic approach with which he had appeared to sympathize in his earlier *De jure praedae* ("On the Law of Booty") and in accordance with which even the content of natural law was understood to be grounded in the mandates of a legislating divine will.[11] In the later work, it should be noted, he distinguishes from the natural law which is made known to us by reason what he calls "volitional divine law," that is, the law that proceeds from "the free will of God" and is conveyed to us by means of revelation. And he does so on the grounds that this "volitional divine law does not enjoin or forbid those things which in themselves and by their own nature are obligatory or impermissible, but [rather] by forbidding things it makes them unlawful, and by commanding it makes them obligatory."[12] "The law of nature," he says (quoting Philo Judaeus to the effect that it is a law that is "immortal" and "incorruptible"), is on the other hand "a dictate of right reason, which points out that an act, according as it is or is not in conformity with rational nature, has in it a quality of moral baseness or moral necessity," and, as a result of that and necessarily so, is "forbidden or enjoined by the author of nature, God." "Measureless as is the power of God," he is powerless to change that law of nature. Just as he "cannot cause that two times two should not make four, so He cannot cause that which is intrinsically evil [to] not be evil." Hence, he arrives at the claim that such a natural law would bind us even if there were no God.[13]

This clear distinction between the natural law and divine "volitional" law is, then, the most appropriate context in which to attempt an understanding of what Grotius intended when he invoked the impious hypothesis. It served for him to emphasize the unchanging character of natural law and the inability even of God to alter or transcend it.[14] But if, among his contemporaries, the Spanish scholastic Francisco Suarez followed a not dissimilar intellectual trajectory from a more voluntarist to a more (though not purely) rationalist or intellectualist understanding of the ultimate grounding of the natural law,[15] others were a good deal less nuanced in their handling of the issue, revealing no comparable hesitation and betraying no comparable vacillation when it came to committing firmly to one side of the equation or the other. Indeed, the dialectic between the two competing positions was to continue on across the whole of the seventeenth century and well into the eighteenth. Thus the voluntarist position, firmly enunciated by Hobbes and (though perhaps more disputably) by Locke, too, was projected forward into the eighteenth century especially by Samuel Pufendorf and (in modified form) by his pupil Christian Thomasius, when it was to encounter stern opposition from the intellectualist point of view at the hands first of Leibniz and then, later on in the century, of Christian Wolff.[16]

In the sharp criticism he directed against Pufendorf's voluntarism (he reproves him in one place for being a muddled Thrasymachus), and moved by his own warmly Platonist sympathies, Leibniz reached back to Plato's *Euthyphro,* the first of the four dialogues focusing on the trial and death of Socrates. In that dialogue, which treats of the essence of piety or holiness, Socrates seeks to maneuver Euthyphro into a dialectical corner from which there can be no escape without conceding the fundamental point that the holy is not holy because the gods love it; the gods instead having to be viewed as loving the holy because of its essential holiness.[17]

For Leibniz, the analogy with the metaphysical grounding of natural law was clear. "It is agreed," he says, "that whatever God wills is [indeed] good and just. But there remains the question whether [as Hobbes and Pufendorf claim] it is good and just because God wills it or whether God wills it because it is good and just; in other words, whether justice and goodness are arbitrary or whether they belong to the necessary and eternal truths about the nature of things, as do numbers and proportions."[18] And, for him, the answer to that question is equally clear. Goodness and justice are "eternal" or "necessary truths," like the truths of mathematics embedded in the divine mind and, as such, the object of the divine understanding. So they are not, as Descartes appears to believe, "arbitrary" and dependent on the divine will.[19] That being so, and the human mind being an image of the divine mind "capable of knowing the system of the universe, and of imitating something of it by architectonic patterns," human minds are also "capable of entering into a kind of society with God," so that God and men are entangled in the same web of morality. Or, as Leibniz himself put it, there is a "common community of justice" between God and men, grounded in "the eternal [and shared] rules of wisdom and justice," a community wherein "universal right is the same for God and men."[20]

That this should be so of the men and inner-worldly divinities of Plato's cosmos is perfectly comprehensible, participants by reason as they alike were in the independent and eternally subsistent forms, archetypes, or ideas of goodness and justice. But the philosophical and theological challenge, of course, is a good deal more testing when the divinity in question, as for Leibniz, was the biblical creator God of might and power, and when what was at stake, therefore, was the very viability of the patristic and scholastic commitment to wedding that notion of God to the Platonic doctrine of forms or ideas. Leibniz, then, might well have done better to forget about the *Euthyphro* and extend his own backward glance no further into the past than to the medieval debate concerning the dimensions of that very challenge. Later on, certainly, his intellectual soulmate, Christian Wolff, saw the debate between rationalists and voluntarists concerning the source or grounding of natural law — still ongoing in the mid-eighteenth century — as analogous to and even continuous with the realist-nominalist dispute of the Middle Ages. He himself affirmed his adhesion to "the scholastic belief in a *moralitas intrinseca et objectiva* [an intrinsic and objective morality], which stems from the *fons* [source] of human reason." And he explicitly acknowledged his own indebtedness in metaphysics to the teaching of Thomas Aquinas.[21]

More than a century earlier Francisco Suarez had adopted a similar stance. In his *De legibus ac deo legislatore* he had helpfully and influentially (though sometimes tendentiously) described the competing positions and set forth the rival apostolic successions, as it were, of medieval scholastic thinkers who had advocated one or the other position. His chosen representatives of the voluntarist position were the nominalist or quasi-nominalist theologians William of Ockham and Pierre d'Ailly from the fourteenth century, along with Jean Gerson and Andreas de Novocastro from the fifteenth.[22] And, later on in the century, it was at Ockham, d'Ailly, and Novocastro, again, though with them also Descartes, that the Cambridge Platonist Ralph Cudworth was to point an accusatory finger when he signaled his alarm at the recrudescence in his own day of the voluntarist ethic. That deplorable ethic, he said, had "crept up in the scholastic age," "promoted and advanced by such as think nothing so essential to the Deity as uncontrollable power and arbitrary will," and teaching "that there is no act evil but as it is prohibited by God, and which cannot be made good if it be commanded by God." In light of what we had to say in the second chapter, what is interesting about Cudworth's particular statement is not simply his identification of the leading late medieval voluntarists. After all, he may conceivably have got that from Suarez. More interesting is his linking of the renewed vogue of the voluntarist theory with the renewal in his own day of what he calls "the physiological hypotheses of Democritus and Epicurus" (i.e., forms of atomism) and with their successful application "to the solving of some of the phenomena of the visible world" (i.e., contemporary scientific endeavor).[23] However debatable, this suggestion may serve to remind us (should that indeed be necessary) that natural law theories are by no means insulated from changes in the temperature and pressure of natural philosophy and scientific thinking, but reflect or presuppose congruent concepts of nature. And it may serve also to fuel the expectation that the configuration of moral and juridical natural law thinking from the thirteenth to the seventeenth centuries will conform to the intellectual template established by the development of the concept of physical laws of nature during that same period, and manifesting a crucial shift from an understanding of the natural order cognate to Whitehead's doctrine of immanent laws of nature to one affiliated with his doctrine of imposed laws.

II

So far as Aquinas is concerned, the fit is gratifyingly close. Arguing, it will be recalled, that law is "something pertaining to reason (*aliquid rationis*)," and that the divine "reason" which governs "the community of the universe" itself possesses "the nature of [an eternal] law," he concluded that in that law "all things in some manner participate ... [deriving] from it certain inclinations to those actions and aims which are proper to them." The eternal law, then, directs to their appropriate end all entities which participate in "the ... community of the universe," all created beings, therefore, in the world of physical nature. And included, of course, are human beings, insofar, that is, as they are natural objects. If, in a fit of perfectly understandable exasperation, you were to rise in your wrath, lay hands on me, and hurl me out of the window, projecting me, therefore, into midair, then my body, being by nature a dull, gross, and earthy thing, would naturally strive, Aristotelian fashion, to reach its proper place in the universe — and that means the center of the earth. I would therefore fall, in so doing revealing my subjection as a body to what we would call a law of (physical) nature but which, for Aquinas, is the eternal law emanating from the divine reason. For God, he says, is related to the world of which he is a creator and ruler as an artist is related to his work. As in the mind of every artist there pre-exists the idea or plan of the work to be produced, so also in every ruler there likewise pre-exists the idea or pattern of the order to be followed by those being governed. Hence, there is what he calls the eternal law — *eternal* because "the divine reason conceives no idea in time"; *law*, because what is involved is "the idea of the divine wisdom" insofar as it moves "all things to their due end."[24]

Human beings, however, are something more than bodies. As bodies, they are indeed subject to the eternal law in the same way as other created beings, animate as well as inanimate. But as "rational creatures," Aquinas says, they are "subject to divine Providence in a more excellent way" than are other creatures, since they are "themselves made participators in Providence itself, in that they control their own actions and the actions of others." For, he continues, "they have . . . a certain share in the divine reason itself, from which they derive a natural inclination to such [moral] actions and ends as are fitting." And the term *natural law* he reserves for this "participation in the Eternal Law by rational creatures."[25]

Aquinas's position, then, amounts basically to this: that there is an eternal law, an immanent order guiding all created things to their appointed ends emanating from the divine ideas, forms, archetypes, or patterns in accordance with which God created those things. Insofar as it concerns man as such — created in his very essence as a rational, moral being, participant by his god-like reason in the divine idea of the good, co-member with God (to use Leibniz's language) in "a common community of justice," caught up alike in a common web of morality — thus far, the *eternal law* is called the *natural law*. To these two categories Aquinas adds two further ones: *divine positive law*, the decrees of God which supplement the natural law and are made known to us by revelation rather than reason;[26] and *human positive law*, the laws enacted by rulers for their subjects.[27] Finally, law being "a rational ordering of things for the common good," he maintains that every human positive law "has the quality of law only insofar as it proceeds from right reason," that is to say, only "to the extent to which [it] . . . derive[s] from natural law."[28]

Aquinas's doctrine of moral or juridical natural law, then, does indeed conform to the template constituted by his thinking concerning the order of physical nature, and it emerges as something that at least approximates to Whitehead's doctrine of laws of nature as immanent and springing from the very nature of things. But what, then, of William of Ockham and his nominalist sympathizers in the fourteenth and fifteenth centuries? Do their views on the matter also parallel their thinking about the order of physical nature, thereby approximating closely this time to Whitehead's doctrine of laws of nature as imposed from without?

In terms of Whitehead's "speculative" approach and of the inner logic of ideas, it would seem, of course, that they should. Whether prompted by strict logical entailment or looser intellectual affinity, the sinuous interconnections among positions adopted in natural theology, epistemology, natural, moral, and legal philosophy would strongly suggest that the intensity of Ockham's focus on the divine freedom and omnipotence and his concomitant preoccupation with the radical contingency of all created forms of order should have led him to affirm in the moral no less than the physical realm something akin to Whitehead's *imposed* doctrine of natural law. But here, alas, the plot thickens. Before one's startled eyes an alarming gap would appear to open up between "should" and "did," suggesting that "scholarship," in Whitehead's terminology, may well be turning out to be on a collision course with "speculation." The trouble, of course, is that Ockham never developed a systematic ethics, and what he did have to say on the matter has always confronted commentators with a formidable challenge. It is only over the course of the past half century, moreover, that the bulk of his writings have for the first time been made available in readily accessible critical editions. As a result, scholarly revisionism has flourished. So far as the interpretation of his ethical teaching goes, consensus has proved to be elusive. The nature and status of his natural law thinking, always contested, has now come to be very much of a disputed question, with a startling range of interpretations being canvassed, some of them, indeed, mutually contradictory.[29]

Thus, at one end of the spectrum, it is argued that insofar as Ockham grounded the norms of justice and the canons of right and wrong in the direct mandates of an unfettered and incomprehensible divine will, he can hardly be said to have had any meaningful doctrine of natural law at all.[30] At the same time, though at the other end of the spectrum, we encounter claims to the effect that there is a "discontinuity between Ockham's philosophical and political thinking," or that his political ideas "...in their great outlines could have been developed...from any of the classical metaphysics of the thirteenth century," or even that "Occam held to the time-honored ancient and medieval tradition of eternal, immutable principles of nature, discoverable by the use of reason," and that there is "no really essential difference...between Occam and Aquinas on this point." So that, in effect, "it is on the whole erroneous to extend the nominalistic-realistic schism to embrace their respective theories of natural law."[31]

Situated, moreover, in the interpretative space that stretches between these extremes is a position that has played an influential role in the currently very lively debate concerning the origins of the notion of subjective or individual natural rights, one that attributes to Ockham a pioneering role in the emergence of that notion, long assumed to have surfaced no earlier than the seventeenth century. That claim, however, is at once complex, important, and different enough to warrant its own separate treatment, and I will return to it in chapter 4. That duly signaled, I propose to limit myself now to an analysis of the central tension between those who, concentrating on the theological voluntarism of Ockham's academic writings, question whether he can truly be said to be a natural law thinker at all, and those who, responding to the political and polemical writings of his later years, conclude that the nominalist and voluntarist commitments of the earlier academic works did not carry over into those later political writings in which he invoked natural law in much the same way as those traditional rationalists who embraced one or another form of metaphysical essentialism.

III

Let me concede at the outset that the tension in question is not lightly to be dismissed. It is underlined by the fact that in Ockham's academic writings — the *Commentary on the Sentences of Peter Lombard* and the *Quodlibetical Questions* — where he addresses ethical matters in a theological and philosophical setting, he refrains from using the language of natural law, whereas in his later political and polemical writings, especially the massive *Dialogus* and *Opus nonaginta dierum*, he freely invokes it.[32] That contrast, moreover, is further dramatized by the seemingly conflicting positions hammered out in those two disparate sets of writings. Texts which link natural law with evident natural reason are broadcast throughout the *Dialogus,* and that law, in its most fundamental mode and as "the natural dictate of reason,"[33] is said to be absolute, immutable, and admitting of no dispensation.[34] In the earlier academic writings, on the other hand, we encounter a long series of texts which enunciate an essentially voluntaristic position in terms which would appear to admit of no equivocation. For the Ockham of these works, it seems clear, "only the divine being is necessary" and "every moral dictate," accordingly, is contingent — dependent, that is — on the unfettered will of God. That will, therefore, is "the only immutable and objective standard of morality," and obedience to it "the only stable and subjective criterion of goodness."[35] And that point Ockham drives home with the famous (or infamous) assertion that robbery, adultery, even hatred of God, all such vices could be stripped of their evil and rendered meritorious "if they were to agree with the divine precept just as now *de facto* their opposites agree with the divine precept."[36] For "evil is nothing other than the doing of something opposite to that which one is obliged to do."[37] And God, who of his freedom and omnipotence is himself "obliged to the causing of no act,"[38] is the ultimate and unchallengeable source of that moral obligation.

A great gulf would appear to yawn, then, between the voluntarist moral teaching affirmed in these theological and philosophical writings of Ockham's academic years and the seemingly rationalist ethic assumed by the natural law talk of his later political writings. And this gives credence to those who have worried that Ockham may (confusingly) be the proponent not of one but of two disparate ethical positions,[39] still more to those who have forthrightly insisted on the simple lack of interconnection between his basic philosophical and theological commitments, on the one hand, and, on the other, the legal and political positions he staked out in the latter years of his life.[40]

This is not, surely, a happy prospect, and certainly not one, I suspect, that would have brought much cheer to a Whitehead in his more persistently speculative moments. The distinguished Ockham scholar Philotheus Boehner derided as "an adventure," it is true, any attempt to derive Ockham's political ideas from what he referred to as his "so-called Metaphysics," and few scholars now would even be tempted to make any truly sweeping claims to that effect.[41] Nonetheless, Georges de Lagarde was right in insisting that to assume Ockham the political thinker to have forgotten his own fundamental philosophical convictions would be "to render a curious homage" to a thinker whose rigorous logic has been so much admired. Nor was Boehner, in the end, unwilling to admit that there were some "inner connections," between the two phases of his thought.[42] And the connection which first suggests itself, the bridge, as it were, over these particular troubled waters, is such, surprisingly, as to nudge one into classifying Ockham in his fundamental philosophical ethics no less than in his later natural law thinking, after all, as belonging ultimately not to the voluntarist but to the rationalist camp.

How could that be? Well, it is clear enough in the *Dialogus* that Ockham aligns the moral prescriptions of natural law with that evident natural reason which, he insists, "in no case fails." But something similar, it turns out, applies to the moral norms analyzed in his academic writings, territory we have portrayed thus far as dominated exclusively by the mandates of an inscrutable divine will. It is time now shamefacedly to confess that that portrayal has been misleadingly incomplete, excluding, as it does, the fact that in those writings Ockham also proffers "a theory of right reason as a source of principles which can direct human action" — a cognate, if you wish, to the strand of natural law thinking woven into the texture of the *Dialogus* and other political writings of his.[43] For an act to be morally good, he tells us, two conditions are necessary. First, it must fall under the power of the will and be willed freely; second, it must be willed in accord with the dictate of right reason. So that "no act is perfectly virtuous unless the will by that act wills that which is dictated by right reason," and does so precisely "because it is dictated by right reason."[44]

So far, so good. There clearly is some sort of bridge between the philosophical ethic embedded in Ockham's academic writings and the natural law ethic that informs the later political works. But before we conclude that it is a thoroughgoing rationalism that constitutes that bridge, we have to ask what then would become of the voluntarist strand in his ethical teaching which, as we have seen, would appear to commit him to the view that "the will of God is the highest norm of morality?"[45] And when we pursue *that* issue, we find that there is more than rationalism to the bridge in question. Push on to the end of the argument and we come face to face with the fact that it is not right reason but the divine will that provides the ultimate grounding of morality and natural law. In the event, important as it is, it turns out that there is nothing final about right reason. If, indeed, no act elicited against right reason can be virtuous, that is the case, Ockham insists, because "such an act would be elicited against the divine precept and against the divine will commanding that such an act be elicited in conformity with right reason." In effect, and the point is decisive, it is "by the very fact that the divine will wills [or commands] it, that right reason dictates what is to be willed" by man.[46] We would appear now to be at the very heart of Ockham's position as it is set forth in his academic writings, and there is no dichotomy between the respective criteria of human right reason and divine preceptive will, which are linked here, and linked significantly and hierarchically.

The case, therefore, for the voluntarist interpretation of morality and, as a result, of natural law would now appear to be watertight. But it is still possible to feel a certain dissatisfaction with this outcome. It may well be true, as we have seen, that in his academic writings Ockham had made right reason itself dependent, for the very role it plays in morality, upon the will of God. But in the *Dialogus* he not only based natural law upon right reason; he asserted also that natural law is absolute, immutable, and admitting of no dispensation. Does not natural law, so derived, shatter the voluntarist framework that we may be guilty of clamping, perhaps somewhat arbitrarily, upon it? Can we really conceive of a moral order as being absolute, immutable, and admitting of no dispensation if it is, indeed, completely dependent on the will of the divine sovereign?

All, however, is not lost, and I say that for two reasons. First, because in the *Dialogus* itself no less than in the *Sentences* Ockham made clear his commitment to the view that the principles of right reason and, therefore, of the natural law are themselves in the power of God. He does so by extending the concept of divine law, or direct divine command to cover the whole of natural law; "every natural law," he says, is "contained explicitly or implicitly in the divine Scriptures."[47] And the Scriptures reveal also that God is capable of ordering "what would *otherwise* be irrational or wrong [and, therefore, contrary to natural law] if it were not done in obedience to divine command."[48] Second, as A. S. McGrade has recently argued, it may also plausibly be claimed that Ockham viewed the dictates of natural law as themselves being *indirect* or "tacit" divine commands. If their content is mediated to us by natural reason, natural reason is not to be viewed as somehow independent of God's overriding power. God, after all, is the creator or author of nature, and had he created "a world with different laws of nature in the physicist's or biologist's sense" our obligations under the natural law would have been different.[49] And as this second reason strongly suggests, it is time now to draw into the discussion the crucial scholastic distinction between God's power conceived as absolute and ordained. That distinction, as we saw in the last chapter, was deployed in the later Middle Ages in an effort to vindicate the freedom and omnipotence of God and the concomitant dependence of the order of physical nature on his will, while at the same time, on the grounds of his faithfulness to his promise or covenant, affirming the *de facto* stability of the particular order he has actually chosen to institute.[50] That that distinction was as pertinent to Ockham's ethical and natural law teaching as we saw it to be to his natural philosophy is indicated by the degree to which that teaching is punctuated, both in his *Sentences* and *Quodlibetical Questions* and in his later political and polemical writings, by such qualifying phrases as "by the common law," "in the present order," "given the divine ordination," "given the ordination which now exists," or "according to the laws ordained and instituted by God," and so on.[51] Of his absolute power — that is, without taking into account the moral order he has actually established — God *could* indeed render good and meritorious acts which by his ordained power he has forbidden. For acts are good and just or bad and unjust, not by their essential nature but simply because God has enjoined or forbidden them. By that ordained power, however, he has actually established a moral order to which right reason is our unfailing guide. When Ockham speaks, then, of a natural law which is absolute, immutable, and admitting of no dispensation, it should be recognized that he is thinking within the framework established by God's ordained power. Thus it is that he can tell us that "in the present order, no act is perfectly virtuous unless elicited in conformity with right reason," and can speak of an act of will which is "intrinsically and necessarily virtuous, given the divine ordination currently prevailing."[52] When, therefore, it comes to determining whether or not Ockham's teaching on moral or juridical natural law is indeed voluntarist and aligned with the template constituted by his views on the order of physical nature (it *is* voluntarist and *is* so aligned), his use of such crucial qualifications as "in the present order" or "given the ordination which now exists" can be, and has been, ignored only at the price of severe misunderstanding.

IV

At the outset of this book I said that I would be advancing three principal arguments. First, that much of the variety in natural law thinking down through the centuries, as well as much of the confusion and ambiguity attendant upon it, reflects the different ways in which the nature of nature has been conceived, the different ways in which the constitutive moment of law has been understood, and the differing ways in which natural law theorists have defined the boundaries of the community of being they view as being subject to the sway of natural law — whether or not, especially, they extend it to embrace the world of nonrational or inanimate nature. Second, that the most important break or discontinuity in the understanding of natural law over the course of the past thousand years, reflecting a shift in the way in which the metaphysical grounding of natural law was understood, occurred in the fourteenth century. As a result, not one but two principal, competing traditions of natural law were handed on from the later Middle Ages to the natural law thinkers of the sixteenth, seventeenth, and eighteenth centuries, helping shape thereby the formidably complex jurisprudential disputes of those centuries. Third, that it was concerns pertaining to natural or philosophical theology that were responsible for engineering that shift. And I also said that I was taking simply for granted the basic assumption that when it came to understanding the intellectual developments of the early modern centuries, the traditional periodization of European history into ancient, medieval, and modern was more of a hindrance than a help.

While I hope that what I have had to say has succeeded in lending some credence to that assumption and to those claims, perhaps, before turning to the rather different (if affiliated) topic of natural rights, I may be permitted a final attempt to drive the point home by adducing two further supportive illustrations. Among the fellow travelers of Ockham in the deplorable advocacy of a voluntarist ethic, Ralph Cudworth, it will be recalled, had fingered the late-fourteenth-century scholastic theologian, Pierre d'Ailly[53] — and, it turns out, with good reason. That it is impossible for a rational creature to sin either by deed or omission against the will of God and not at the same time against the dictate of reason or the law of nature or of some other created law — that d'Ailly is perfectly willing to concede, always provided, of course, that one is speaking of the moral order presently prevailing and established by God's ordained power (*potentia ordinata*), for, by God's absolute power (*potential absoluta*), it is quite

possible to sin against the divine will and yet in no way to contravene the dictate of reason or the law of nature.[54] Important
as the role of reason and of natural law in morality undoubtedly
is, there is nothing final about right reason, and the implication
follows that if, of his absolute power, God were to will otherwise,
right reason could lose its proud role as the natural sign of God's
obligating law. Here the parallel between the order of (physical)
nature and that of morality is firmly drawn. If in the natural
order presently prevailing "every secondary cause ... produces its
effect of its very nature (*ex natura rei*)" we must not forget that
that secondary cause is itself a cause not because of its nature
but "solely because of the will of God," who, in choosing of his
ordained power to limit himself to producing some natural effect
by means of a secondary cause, "not only produces that effect, but
also makes the secondary cause to be the cause of that effect,"[55]
just as, for example, and there being no contradiction involved,
he could produce in us an intuition of a nonexisting object.[56] And
being similarly "the first obligating law in the genus of obligating law," he could likewise by his absolute power oblige a rational
creature directly by himself and without recourse to the sort of
created law (natural or divine) to which, of his ordained power,
he limits himself in imposing such an obligation.[57] Indeed, the
prescriptions of all such created laws (natural no less than divine)
being radically contingent on his will, he could of his absolute
power even make it meritorious to hate God, since he can do
anything that does not involve a contradiction, and since acts are
good and just or bad and unjust not of their own intrinsic nature
or essence but simply because God has enjoined or forbidden
them.[58]

And, for the second illustration, I should like to reach ahead
into the seventeenth century and to draw it from none other than
John Locke, who has usually been viewed (though not, of course,

by Leo Strauss) as a significant spokesman for the natural law tradition. And I draw it from what he had to say in the seventh of his early *Essays on the Law of Nature*. The text in question has sometimes been used either to establish that Locke in his natural law thinking wavered inconsistently between a voluntarist and an intellectualist position or, more sweepingly, to prove that his teaching was ultimately an intellectualist one.[59] But let me suggest it would lend itself to neither of those uses if one chose to approach it — as, happily, some Locke commentators are now beginning to recommend — with the late medieval voluntarist tradition in mind, the dialectic between omnipotence and covenant characteristic of that tradition, and with the use made accordingly of the distinction between God's power conceived as absolute and ordained.

In my second chapter I argued that that covenantal tradition is the appropriate context in which to attempt an understanding of the physico-theological views espoused by such luminaries of the new scientific thinking as Gassendi, Charleton, and Boyle, people writing in Locke's own lifetime and with whom, it should be noted, Leibniz was inclined to group him.[60] It should be noted, too, that some recent commentators on Locke have come to the conclusion that "it is probably impossible to overestimate the primacy...of [his] ...theism for his whole account of the natural and moral order," have stressed his preoccupation with the divine omnipotence, and have insisted that there is, in effect, "a symmetry," at once both epistemological and ontological, "between...[his]...moral theory and his philosophy of science," between, therefore, his notions of natural law in the moral order and laws of nature in the physical world.[61] If the latter have what Locke calls a "constant and regular connexion in the ordinary course of Things," they lack the absolute necessity that pertains to mathematical propositions and have therefore, he says, to be attributed to "nothing else, but...the arbitrary Will and Good Pleasure of the Wise Architect."[62] This is true, similarly, of his notion of natural law in the moral order, which is also grounded firmly in the divine will. At the same time, both laws, moral as well as physical, that God has actually chosen to ordain are to be understood as a good deal more than fleeting contingencies. They are, indeed, *laws,* and they reflect and guarantee the existence of a stable order that possesses at least a conditional or hypothetical necessity—what Michael Ayers labels in a happy formulation as a necessity that is "hypothetical but hard."[63]

In his seventh *Essay on the Law of Nature,* then, and speaking of the moral or juridical natural law, Locke says that "the bonds of this law are perpetual and coeval with the human race, beginning with it and perishing with it at the same time." Asserting thus the existence of a "harmony" between natural law and man's rational nature, he goes on to elucidate that claim by asserting that natural law does not "depend on an unstable and changeable will, but on the eternal order of things." For "certain essential features of things are immutable, and certain duties arise out of necessity and cannot be other than they are."[64]

Of course, if one chose to isolate that last statement and to ignore Locke's earlier alignment of the perpetuity and binding force of natural law with the historical existence of the human species, it would be easy to take him as making more sweepingly intellectualist claims than he actually is. What I would suggest, instead, is that his position is cognate to that which Ockham took when he spoke of natural law as being absolute, immutable, and admitting of no dispensation. As with Ockham (or, for that matter, d'Ailly), what could easily be taken to be an unambiguously intellectualist position is subject to a crucial qualification. As with Ockham (or d'Ailly), that qualification extends to the moral no less than the natural order. As with Ockham (or d'Ailly), the type of necessity he has in mind (and as he goes on to make quite clear) is not an absolute, but rather a contingent, hypothetical, or conditioned necessity, one which depends in effect on the particular choice God has made, and one that reflects, therefore, the balancing of omnipotence with covenant and promise. "God *could have created men,*" Locke concedes, "such that they would be without eyes, and not need them." But he did not choose so to act. As a result, "so long as they [men] use their eyes and want to open them, and so long as the sun shines, they must of necessity come to know the alternations of day and night, be aware of the differences of colors," and so on. Similarly, though on the ethical front now, "*since man has been made such as he is,* equipped with reason and his other faculties and destined for this mode of life, there necessarily results from his inborn constitution some definite duties for him, which cannot be other than they are." If "this natural duty *will never be abolished,*" it is not simply because (being subject to it) "human beings cannot alter this law," but also

> because God certainly *would not wish to do so.* For since, according to His infinite and eternal wisdom, He has made man such that these duties of his necessarily follow from his very nature, He surely will not alter what has been made and create a new race of men, who would have another law and moral rule, seeing that natural law stands and falls together with the nature of man *as it is at present.*[65]

Thus, just as in relation to the world of nature and because it would involve no contradiction, God *could,* in the absoluteness of his power and by what Locke refers to as one of those "extraordinary effects [that]...we call miracles," "put out of its ordinary course some phenomena of this great world" or even "create another world separate wholly from this,"[66] so, too, by changing human nature itself could he abrogate the natural law as it is presently constituted. But "could" is not the same as "will." No contradiction, after all, is involved in omnipotency's choosing to bind itself. God is, indeed, a "holy, just and righteous God," and as Locke in his *Two Treatises* twice reminds those who seek to emancipate princes from the bonds of the law, even God, his freedom and power notwithstanding, condescends to "tye Himself with oaths and promises."[67]

If the Locke who emerges from this reading of his complex and sometimes unclear statements about natural law is unquestionably a latter-day voluntarist, he is, then, a voluntarist of the late medieval stamp whose thinking witnesses to the great shift Ockham and his voluntarist successors had engineered in the fourteenth and fifteenth centuries. His emphasis on the divine omnipotence is, accordingly, so modulated as to accommodate a firm commitment to the existence of an order — natural, moral, and also, indeed, salvational — seemingly intellectualist in nature, but actually grounded in divine will, choice, promise, and covenant. It conforms, in effect, to the intellectual template established by the development of physical laws of nature from the thirteenth to the seventeenth century and manifesting an historic shift to an understanding of the natural order cognate to Whitehead's doctrine of imposed laws. We are left, then, to ascertain if or how the emergence of the notion of natural rights to such prominence on the modern intellectual scene relates to this sinuous pattern of development. That task I will address in my fourth and final chapter.

Four

NATURAL RIGHTS
Origins and Grounding

"Natural Rights," Kenneth Minogue once memorably asserted, "are as modern as the internal combustion engine."[1] A refreshingly forthright claim, and if clarity were to be viewed as the supreme virtue one would have to concede that the quality of discourse about the origins and development of the concept of natural rights has certainly gone downhill in the quarter century since he made it. It is true that the clamor of rights-talk or talk about the history of theories concerning subjective natural or human rights has now become so insistent as to threaten to clog the scholarly arteries available to it.[2] And the analytic complexity of that talk is immediately evident. In the seventeenth century, insisting that "law, and right, differ as much as obligation, and liberty," Hobbes stipulated the need to insert a fundamental distinction between "a LAW OF NATURE, *lex naturalis,*" which "is a precept or general rule, found out by reason, by which a man is forbidden to do that, which is destructive of his life," and "the RIGHT OF NATURE, which writers commonly call *jus naturale,*" and which "is the liberty each man hath, to use his own power, as he will himself, for the preservation of his own nature."[3] And, focusing on the latter, or subjective, meaning of natural right, subsequent commentators have introduced a whole battery of additional refinements. The most important of these is the distinction "within moral-philosophical discourse" between, on the one hand, "'liberty-rights' ('active rights'), independent licenses of action...which can be seen as constituting an area wherein the individual and her choice are sovereign," and, on the other, "'claim-rights' ('passive rights,' 'rights of recipience') which are dependent for their existence on the obligations of others."[4] Worthy of mention beyond that, moreover, is the celebrated analysis by Wesley Hohfeld, who identified no less than eight fundamental logical relations pertaining to the ways in which the term *right* is used in relation to the individual.[5]

But that sort of analytic rigor notwithstanding, we still have to face the fact that "the history of the western rights tradition remains to be written."[6] Even so far as inquiry into the specific question of origins goes, and that will be my concern in this chapter, the smoke of battle still hangs low over what has become of recent years a rather crowded and confusing field on which competing hypotheses still maneuver warily for advantage.[7] But while the caveats of the historians still seem (surprisingly) to generate no more than pallid harmonics in the thinking of their colleagues in philosophy or political science, one firm conclusion should be stated right at the outset, namely, that the current state of historical research on the matter is no longer such as to warrant the degree of confidence that sustains the calm robustness of Minogue's claim.

In this conflicted realm, then, complexity reigns now as king. What Minogue himself was echoing was the traditional assumption of early modern origins which Leo Strauss and C. B. Macpherson had (in their differing ways) sought classically to vindicate, and which latter-day Straussians continue unabashedly to defend.[8] But the proliferating arguments for one or another earlier point of origin have become too insistent simply to be dismissed. That is true whether the determinative moment of origin is detected in the fifteenth, fourteenth, or twelfth and thirteenth centuries — in the theology of Jean Gerson (thus Richard Tuck), in the nominalism of William of Ockham (thus Georges de Lagarde, Michel Villey, Michel Bastit), in the natural law theory of Thomas Aquinas (thus John Finnis), or, even earlier, in the juristic formulations of the twelfth- and thirteenth-century canon lawyers (thus Brian Tierney, Charles Reid).[9] The scholarly debates on the matter have become exceedingly intricate, and I realize that to those most directly embroiled in them, segmenting the issues as I propose to do may well smack of oversimplification. But segment nonetheless I must, beginning with the classic case for seventeenth-century origins and working my way back, first to the rival case made for fourteenth-century philosophical beginnings, and then to the claims advanced for juristic rather than philosophic origins in the twelfth and thirteenth centuries.

I

If "all civilizations have cherished ideals of justice and right order," it has well been said that "they have not normally expressed those ideals in terms of individual natural rights."[10] To be tempted to do so appears, until the very recent past, to have been a peculiarly Western proclivity. We would be wise to refrain, then, from projecting our own rights-centered views either upon those other civilizations that chose to frame their thinking about a just social order in very different ways, or, for that matter, upon the more distant reaches of the Western past to which, it seems, rights-centered moral discourse was largely alien. Until recently, indeed, it was usual to pinpoint the "classical age" of Hobbes and Locke in the seventeenth century as the era which saw the birth of the concept of natural rights.[11]

That period, it was generally argued (though in differing ways), witnessed the emergence on the English intellectual and political scene of what was later to develop into "the classical variant of the liberal ideology of individual rights."[12] Grounded in a novel species of radical individualism, in the notion that human beings are rights-bearing agents possessed already of freedom in a pre-political state of nature, that ideology went hand in glove with the ascription of a real choice on the part of the autonomous individual will as to whether or not to engage itself in politics. Such generalities were commonplace enough. But Leo Strauss, in the most powerful and influential formulation of the case for seventeenth-century origins, chose to go further.[13]

Using the single term "Natural Right" to comprehend what in English usage are usually designated separately as "natural law" and "natural rights," he constructed an essentially dramatic account of the history of the tradition. Whereas, he said, in terms of the "classical and medieval understanding of 'Natural Right,'" "the fundamental and absolute moral fact" was a duty, the modern version understood it as a right (181). Notwithstanding John Locke's approving (and misleading) evocations in the *Second Treatise* of the essentially Thomistic understanding of the natural law propounded by Richard Hooker, the great Elizabethan Anglican divine, we should not miss the fact that "the notion of natural right had undergone a fundamental change between Hooker and Locke" (165–66). And the great engineer of that "momentous change was Thomas Hobbes — that imprudent, impish, and iconoclastic extremist," who, Locke's judicious silences notwithstanding, exerted a profound influence over him and, for that matter, over "all subsequent modern thought" (166).

What Hobbes in effect did — or so Strauss argued — was to draw out in systematic fashion the political philosophical consequences of two major departures characteristic of the early modern intellectual scene.

The first was Machiavelli's historic reorienting of political thinking concerning "the question of the right order of society" from the classical and medieval preoccupation with "how man *ought* to live" to a modern, "realistic" approach which took its bearings "by how men actually *do* live" (174, italics mine). For "it was Machiavelli, that greater Columbus, who had discovered the continent on which Hobbes... [was later to] erect his structure" (177).

The second major departure was the destruction by the new (Democritan-Epicurean-mechanistic) physical science of the "teleological view of the universe" in which the classical natural right had been embedded and in accordance with which "man's natural end" had been the lodestar by means of which reason could discern how, morally speaking, he should live (7–8, 169–70). And the outcome? Nothing less than the revolutionary reorientation of political philosophy from its long-standing preoccupation with final causes to an adamant focus on efficient causes, from ends or purposes to antecedent events or beginnings, from the notion of man as by nature a social and political being dependent for his very humanity on life in the polis to the conception of the natural man as an autonomous agent dwelling in a pre-political state of nature, driven incessantly by that "most powerful of all passions...the fear of death" (180), and possessed already (and therefore) of that fundamental, inalienable natural right of self-preservation and, with it, the right to decide upon the means conducive to that objective.

Upon that "unconditional and absolute" right, which Strauss described as "the fundamental moral fact" and "the sole root of all justice and morality," hinge all other natural rights. And from it derive all those natural duties which Hobbes portrays as pertaining to what he misleadingly calls "the laws of nature," duties which are "binding only to the extent to which their performance does not endanger our self-preservation" (181). For such laws "are but conclusions, or theorems concerning what conduceth to [one's] . . . conservation and defence."[14] And, overwhelming textual evidence to the contrary, this interpretation Strauss tried to foist also on Locke's natural law thinking, which "can . . . be understood perfectly," he insisted, only if one assimilates it, in effect, to the version he attributed to Hobbes (229).[15]

About Strauss's reading of Hobbes overall there has, of course, been much disagreement,[16] and that disagreement properly extends to his notion that it was Hobbes who was responsible for engineering some sort of Copernican shift from a moral universe revolving around the obligatory and community-oriented prescriptions of the natural law to one centered on the free and individualistic exercise of one's natural rights. A great deal could be said about this, but here, however, space permits the identification of no more than two of the difficulties involved.

The first concerns the alleged subordination from Hobbes onward of duties to rights or, put differently, the derivation or ultimate deduction of the laws of nature from the primary and inalienable individual right of self-preservation. Whatever one makes of Hobbes himself — and to that I will turn in a moment — the fact remains, as Knud Haakonssen has amply demonstrated, that the ties that bound the moral thinking of the seventeenth and eighteenth centuries to the traditional commitments of the past were not so readily severed as Strauss and his followers suggest. In those centuries, "obligation and right" tended to be seen, as Thomas Rutherford was to put it in 1754, "as correlative terms."[17] In the mainstream of eighteenth-century jurisprudence, indeed, natural rights were seen to derive from natural law and natural duty. So that, to most natural law theorists, "moral agency consisted in being subject to natural law and carrying out the duties imposed by such law, whereas rights were derivative, being merely means to the fulfillment of duties."[18]

If that is the case, if, at least in this aspect of natural law thinking, the continuities with the past were indeed so marked as still to sustain into the eighteenth century "a sea of Christian-Stoic or neo-Aristotelian teleology, in which rights remained derivative powers in the service of the duty imposed by natural law,"[19] then the burden of proof on anyone who wishes with Strauss to argue that Hobbes (let alone Locke) succeeded in engineering a decisive break with the old natural law tradition becomes accordingly all the heavier; the more so, and herein lies the second difficulty with Strauss's case, in that in order to sustain it he is obliged to resort to reading between the lines of the texts themselves in accord with the esoteric method of interpretation which he viewed as appropriate for certain types of philosophic writing.[20] That issue I cannot dwell upon here beyond referring to my first chapter and noting again that I myself take Hobbes's more theological moments seriously and am inclined to sympathize, therefore, with the type of interpretative approach, admittedly alien to that of Strauss, but pursued by such as Michael Oakeshott, Willis Glover, Howard Warrender, and, most recently, A. P. Martinich.[21] And that means, of course, that I take Hobbes's definition of law in general as the result of an efficient cause and the mandate of a sovereign will to extend also to natural law, the efficient cause in that case being the omnipotent creator God and the obligating prescription of that law being the mandate of his sovereign will.

All of this aligns well with Hobbes's epistemological nominalism, his parallel political individualism, his mechanistic understanding of reality, and his dismissal from the realm of law and politics as well as from that of nature of those teleological preoccupations characteristic of so many of the great philosophers of the classical and medieval worlds. And all of it aligns well too, and of course, with Whitehead's doctrine of imposed law, one which, as we saw in chapters 2 and 3, had come to the fore among the medieval scholastic philosophers and theologians some three centuries prior to Hobbes, in so doing engineering a fundamental shift in the way in which the nature and grounding of natural law was understood. Insofar, however, as Strauss was highlighting the novelties he was ascribing to Hobbes by playing the latter's views off against medieval as well as classical notions of natural law, it was Thomas Aquinas, not William of Ockham, whom he chose as his point of comparison.[22] And, with Aquinas's views on the matter being clearly aligned with Whitehead's doctrine of immanent laws of nature, Hobbes's position understandably stood out in bold relief.

No such sharp contrast would have been evident had Strauss chosen, instead, to focus as his medieval point of comparison on Ockham, whose voluntarism had much in common with that of Hobbes and Locke. But on Ockham he was silent, and one is led to ask if the alleged shift in emphasis from the prescriptions of natural law to the prerogatives of natural rights, which Strauss quintessentially associates with Hobbes, should be sought instead in the writings of Ockham. And that question, it turns out, has long since been posed (and answered in the affirmative) by those who harbor the conviction that the genesis of the notion of subjective natural rights, the "Copernican moment"[23] in the long and conflicted history of "natural right" had occurred, not in the seventeenth, but already in the fourteenth century.

II

Although Georges de Lagarde in his brilliant *Naissance de l'esprit laïque au déclin du Moyen Age* had earlier pointed in the same direction,[24] it was left to Michel Villey to frame the specific and developed case for fourteenth-century origins that appears (directly or at one or another remove) to have shaped the assumptions on the matter held by a varied array of subsequent commentators, from Heinrich Rommen to Isaiah Berlin, and from Louis Dumont to Michel Bastit.[25] Although Villey was by calling a legal historian and, over a period of forty years, had made a series of substantial contributions to our understanding of classical and medieval jurisprudence,[26] he tended nonetheless to privilege philosophical considerations over the purely jurisprudential and to proceed on the assumption that changes in the latter sphere had to reflect prior and more fundamental shifts in metaphysics.

That point of view he held in common with Strauss. Beyond that, the two men also shared a marked hostility to the modern notion of individual subjective rights — *"cet enfant monstrueux"* is the term Villey used of it.[27] Again, they shared the assumption that that notion's unfortunate emergence *must* have presupposed the subversion of the classical and Thomistic vision of a universe fraught with purpose and intelligibility, with the concomitant loss of any moral or juridical natural law expressing an objective order of justice. And, finally, they shared the firm conviction that the modern notion of individual and subjective rights was wholly incompatible with the "traditional" notion of natural law.[28] So far as the question of origins goes, where their respective diagnoses differed simply concerned the precise moment at which the pernicious infant finally emerged to flex its monstrous limbs.

In his earlier work Villey had probed in somewhat cautious fashion the question of whether or not the notion of subjective

individual rights could be found, at least implicitly, in the classical
Roman jurists. By the late 1950s, however, he had come to the
firm conclusion that "Roman jurists did not conceive of the legal
order as essentially a structure of individual rights in the manner
of some modern ones." Further than that, he had also concluded
that such a conception could not have arisen until Aristotelian and
Stoic conceptions of "an objectively just [and rationally apprehen-
sible] social order" had been abandoned.[29] Moving on, then, in
the early 1960s, from the close scrutiny of juristic texts to an
approach conditioned by broader philosophical concerns, Villey
noted that the early modern political philosophers and legal commentators, notable among them Grotius and Hobbes, had come
to view *jus* (traditionally, right, law, or what is objectively just and
fair, *id quod justum est*) very much as a subjective right, faculty, or
power of action possessed by the individual. And, looking back
at the later Middle Ages, he pinpointed William of Ockham as
the thinker responsible for that novel and intimate association of
power with right and, therefore, for the first "clear and complete
definition of subjective right." Ockham, in effect, he declared to
be "the father of subjective right."[30]

On the face of it, there is something quite plausible and ap-
pealing about that claim. For anyone moved by the presence of
consistent patterns in the history of ideas it suggests, beguilingly,
that the advent of the notion of subjective rights can be (at least
loosely) correlated with the crucial shift on which the two previous chapters have dwelt. That shift, it will be recalled, concerned
the very grounding of natural law and the concomitant emergence
of the pattern of thinking associated with Whitehead's doctrine
of imposed laws of nature. If Villey is correct, then, the fourteenth century emerges yet once more as the pivotal moment in
the reshaping of the natural law tradition.

With that temptingly symmetrical possibility in view, we should note that it is understandable that this particular claim should come from Villey, who was clearly responsive to Georges de Lagarde's philosophically conditioned approach to Ockham's social and political thinking. We have seen that with his nominalistic and de-Platonizing rejection of the doctrine of the divine ideas so deeply entrenched in the thinking of metaphysical essentialists like Aquinas, Ockham had been led to reconceptualize the nature of the universe. He had come to see it as one in which an inscrutable and omnipotent God directly confronts the multiplicity of singular, autonomous, and radically contingent existents he has created and which are capable, should he so will it, of existing independently of one another. Gone, therefore, is the great chain of metaphysical intermediaries so deeply embedded in the thinking of the scholastic essentialists. Gone, too, any idea of "real" relations among existents. Gone, as a result, any apprehension of the order of the universe as something distinct from its multiple existing components. Hence, or so de Lagarde claimed, the social atomism or "individualist microbe" that Ockham introduced into medieval political thinking.[31] Hence, too, according now to Villey, his abandonment of the very "idea of a rational moral law by emphasizing arbitrary divine commands" and his filling of "the resulting void with a body of [subjective] natural rights based on individual wills."[32]

Villey portrayed Ockham as having arrived at this position, not in the philosophical and theological writings of his earlier years, but in the *Opus nonaginta dierum* (1332), one of the polemical works he contributed to the great Franciscan quarrel with the papacy over the doctrine of evangelical poverty.[33] But in so doing, Villey insisted, he was no more than being faithful to the fundamental philosophical intuitions that had served to set him at odds with the "classic philosophy" of an Aristotle or Aquinas. "It is the whole philosophy professed by William of Ockham . . . that is the mother of subjective right."[34] And what he had particularly in mind when he said that is the critical intersection in Ockham's thinking of his nominalism in epistemology and his voluntarism in ethics. From his nominalism, with its insistence that only particulars are possessed of extra-mental reality, flows a way of thinking that revolves around the singular entity and, by extension into the legal realm, around the powers and claims of the individual. And from his voluntarism, with its insistence on the priority of will over reason both in God and in the human creature made in the divine likeness, flows an intense preoccupation with power. "The source of every legal order can only be the will and power of an individual." "If the *first* notion of right . . . is the subjective right of God,"[35] the subjective rights, claims, faculties, or powers of human individuals follow inevitably and in all too short order. They, rather than a concern with what is just and fair in some objective sense, become the point of departure of a system of legal thinking, and Ockham is led, accordingly, in what Villey described as a "semantic shift . . . rich in consequences" to "usurp the term 'natural right' in order to designate something quite other than *authentic* natural right."[36]

What, then, is to be made of this claim, involving as it does the postulation of a break or rupture in the history of natural law thinking no less dramatic than that alleged by Strauss, but with Ockham rather than Hobbes now cast in the role of villain? Much could be said on the matter, and much, indeed, has been said. But I must confine myself to identifying three difficulties which serve, I believe, to undercut the viability of the claim.

First, however sympathetic one may be to the idea that there are indeed some continuities between Ockham's fundamental philosophical and theological commitments and some of the positions he came later in life to adopt in his political and polemical writings (and I am), one has to be sensitive to the fact that such continuities are likely to be very subtle and that any route from epistemological nominalism to legal or political individualism is destined almost certainly to be indirect.[37] It matters, then, that the argument Villey made for that particular link is really quite loose-limbed, grounded, in effect, on an issue where the burden of proof is exceedingly heavy, on little more than reiterated assertion.

Second, the unargued assumption that the notion of the subjective rights of individuals is simply incompatible with the traditional notion of objective natural right, and the concomitant claim that with Ockham the latter simply disappears and is replaced by the former, both carry no more conviction than did Strauss's comparable assumption or the claim he in turn made with regard to Hobbes. So far as Aquinas is concerned, twentieth-century commentators have not always shared Villey's view that his natural law theory was "necessarily exclusive" of or incompatible with the notion of subjective individual rights.[38] Two, indeed, have made powerful cases for the opposed position, arguing that natural rights are either implicit in, or can actually be seen to be grounded in, his natural law teaching.[39] And as for Ockham himself, that he used the language of subjective rights and that he played a significant role in shaping the notion of natural rights is not in dispute.[40] Thus far, in fact, there is something to Villey's claim. But, as we saw in the last chapter,[41] that certainly did not mean that Ockham was led to abandon a commitment to the idea that there exists a natural law accessible to the right reason of all men and prescribing for their living objective moral norms. What his voluntarism entailed was not the abandonment of that traditional commitment to the existence of a natural and objective moral order but, rather, a crucial shift in the understanding of the nature and grounding of that natural order. And that shift was to be fraught with consequences for the natural law tradition as it came down to Hobbes and Locke and as it continued on, indeed, into the eighteenth century.

Third, there is a difficulty more extrinsic in nature, but no less telling for that. Since Villey wrote, scholarly research on the natural rights tradition has made it increasingly clear that, however important Ockham's role may have been as a shaper and transmitter to future ages of the notion of subjective rights, there was nothing particularly novel about his own deployment of that notion. No marked "semantic shift," "Copernican moment," or great upheaval of the philosophic spirit was called for in his day in order to link *jus* with *potestas* and to speak of right as a licit power. Whatever reorientation of thinking and language may have been called for appears to have taken place already, and to have occurred in the realm of juristic rather than philosophic discourse. It appears also to have begun during the great flowering of legal studies that occurred in the twelfth century. In particular, it appears to have taken place in the thinking especially of the canon lawyers on whose work (as has often been remarked)[42] Ockham himself drew so heavily in his political and polemical writings. That being so, the quest for the origins of the notion of subjective natural rights must now take us back further into the Middle Ages and away from what has been traditionally a preoccupation with philosophical authors.

III

The humanistic jurisprudence characteristic of what, since the time of Charles Homer Haskins, we have been accustomed to call the Twelfth-Century Renaissance, has attracted the attention of more than one scholar concerned with the emergence of the notion of subjective rights as well as with ideas closely affiliated with it. Though he did not believe that the critical breakthrough to a clearly articulated version of that notion had occurred prior to Ockham, Villey himself had detected some preliminary and hesitant moves in that direction in the way in which the medieval glossators on the Roman law had handled the concept of *dominium.* So, too, following his lead, had Richard Tuck.[43] So far as the contemporary glossators on the canon law were concerned, moreover, Harold Berman found that in their commentaries on such matters as marriage law and the law of contracts an intriguing emphasis on internal disposition and individual will is evident.[44] Tuck went further than that, but he still insisted that with the canonists, as with the commentators on the Roman civil law, the only type of subjective rights detectable were not those active rights or licenses for action that scholars like Strauss or Villey usually had in mind but, rather, what have variously been called claim-rights or passive rights or rights of recipience.[45] It was left, then, for Brian Tierney and, later, Charles Reid, to find to the contrary that the notion of active rights (and related refinements too) could be detected already in the accumulating mass of glosses or commentaries that the canonists wrote from the twelfth century onwards — both the Decretists or commentators on Gratian's *Decretum* (or *Concord of discordant canons*), the great twelfth-century legal text, and the Decretalists or commentators on the thirteenth- and fourteenth-century collections of papal decretals. The case they have made has proved to be a powerful one, and one certainly deserving of far more attention on the part of those concerned with early modern and modern theories of natural or human rights than it has thus far received.[46]

In some respects, of course, that comparative lack of attention is not altogether surprising. While some of the canonists were clearly legal thinkers of great distinction, the fact remains that the names of even the most prominent among them are still almost unknown today to any but medieval specialists: in the twelfth century, Rufinus, Alanus, Huguccio, even the great Gratian himself; in the thirteenth, Bernard of Parma, Sinibaldo Fieschi (Pope Innocent IV), Guido of Baysio, Hostiensis; in the fourteenth, Johannes Andreae. These are hardly household names, nor are they thinkers who did us the favor of producing specific treatises on rights. Instead, their views on the matter are embedded *seriatim* in their glosses on the *Decretum* and decretals, and some of those glosses have yet to find their way from manuscript into print. Only of recent years, then, have they made any really noticeable appearance in the arena of scholarly debate about rights, and much work remains to be done before their comparative invisibility in that arena can finally be overcome.

That said, and thanks largely to the pioneering work of Tierney and Reid,[47] some things have already become clear. First, the use of *jus* or right to mean a subjective right was a commonplace in twelfth-century canonistic discourse from Gratian himself onward. Further than that, the association of "right" and "power" to which Villey attached so much importance in the thinking of Ockham was equally commonplace at that time. By the end of the same century, moreover, the "modern" distinction between "active" or "liberty-rights" and "passive" or "claim-rights" was firmly in place in decretist commentaries. And during the course of the thirteenth century a canonistic vocabulary of rights had crystallized that comes remarkably close to the set of legal relations that Hohfeld was to identify in twentieth-century rights discourse. In urging that last point Reid is careful to insist that what is involved is not simply a sense of individual rights being embedded *implicitly* in the canonistic legal structure. Something much more specific is involved. "The decretalists," he says, "possessed a well-developed *explicit* understanding of subjective rights." "Large areas of medieval canon law consisted," in fact, "of structures of rights," perhaps none more obviously than matrimonial law, where a firm commitment to the notion of an objective order of right did not preclude an equally firm recognition of the rights which the contraction of a marriage conferred upon the marital partners.[48] So far, then, as one's concern is with the subjective rights of individuals, active no less than passive, and grounded explicitly in the positive law, the pertinent history begins no later than the twelfth century.

That claim, of course, is made of a feudalized and highly legalistic culture in which the task of navigating the rocks and shoals of everyday life required a willingness to assert or respond to complex patterns of customary prerogatives, claims, and rights. But what, in the second place, of the more rarified notion of *natural* rights? Did it, too, rise to the surface during the Middle Ages, or must we await its advent in the seventeenth century? Here, admittedly, the line of argument becomes somewhat more intricate. But here, too, it points to the conclusion that the roots of the concept of natural rights are also engaged in decretist soil. After all, Gratian's *Decretum* itself begins with a challenging set of contrasts between natural law (*jus naturale*) and human mores or (positive) laws that proved problematic enough to catch early on the attention of the glossators.[49] No sooner did they sink their interpretative teeth into the text than a terminological shift becomes evident. It involves a slippage from Gratian's own consistent use of *jus naturale* to denote an objective body of moral law (i.e., *lex naturalis*) toward a more subjective usage. Huguccio of Pisa (d. 1210), for example, not only distinguished between the objective and subjective usages, but also asserted as primary the subjective use of *jus naturale* to denote "a [natural] force of the [individual] soul." And other Decretist glossators were soon interpreting *jus* as a power (*potestas*) or faculty (*facultas*) to act—what, in effect, we today would label as an active subjective right.[50]

Across the course of the thirteenth and fourteenth centuries, moreover, via an appeal to the mandates of natural law, a whole body of particular subjective rights ranging from procedural rights, marital rights, and property rights to the right of defending oneself or consenting to one's ruler came to be defended as natural rights. But it was the bitter fourteenth-century dispute between Pope John XXII and the leadership of the Franciscan Order concerning the doctrine of evangelical poverty that first drew the concept of subjective natural rights "into the center of a major public debate involving a reigning pope and some of the leading intellectuals of the day," Ockham himself included. That dispute, in turn, was to serve as a kind of ideological relay station, picking up the canonistic signal on rights, ridding it of inherited incidental static, broadcasting it in purified and amplified form to other realms of discourse (philosophical and theological as well as legal), and forwarding it onto the receptors of future ages.[51]

Thus, in the course of that dispute, John XXII argued against the established Franciscan distinction between the ownership (*dominium*) and the simple use (*usus facti*) of goods and, accordingly, against the Order's assertion that neither individually nor in common did the friars possess *dominium* over the goods they used. He did so by denying outright the legal validity, when applied to goods that are consumed by use, of the very distinction between ownership and use. He did so, too, by condemning as heretical the then recent assertion by the Franciscan general chapter at Perugia (1322) that Christ and the Apostles owned no property either individually or collectively. In the course of responding to the papal onslaught by insisting that it was precisely in imitation of the life of Christ and the Apostles that the friars renounced all property both individually and collectively, retaining only the "simple use" of things,[52] Ockham was led to assert that far from conferring any proprietary right on Adam and Eve in the state of innocence, God had endowed them only with a "power of using" the consumables they needed for food and drink. Not only (*pace* John XXII) could that "simple use" exist without entailing ownership, it was, further than that, a *natural* right, indeed an inalienable natural right.[53]

In subsequent works, moreover, (the *Dialogus* and *Breviloquium*), Ockham was destined to move on from this very particular evocation of a natural right to make use of the consumables needed to sustain life itself to a broader and more "political" appeal to the natural right of a people to choose its ruler and, further, to the limitation of the power of that ruler (whether papal or imperial) by the natural rights inherent in his subjects.[54] And, by an exceedingly complex process of transmission, involving successive refinements and incremental change, such ideas were to find their way, via the writings of jurists and theologians alike, all the way down to the "classic age" of natural rights discourse in the seventeenth century, with Jean Gerson in the fifteenth century and the great Spanish scholastics in the sixteenth looming especially large on the way.

Of course, how exactly to reconstruct the history of that process of transmission is likely for some time to come to remain a bone of scholarly contention.[55] On that score, much detailed work remains to be done. But what is already, and in the third place, perfectly clear, is that the process involved is not one marked by discontinuities of the sort canvassed by Villey, still less by dramatic, ahistorical, and quasi-Foucauldian ruptures of the kind urged by Strauss. Instead, the outlines of a more credible alternative account have now begun to emerge. And what they suggest is a slow, evolutionary development of natural rights talk originating in what has well been called "the great sea of medieval jurisprudence" (Tierney), but interacting eventually with the philosophy and theology of the later Middle Ages and of the second (sixteenth century) scholasticism, finding its way thence into the philosophical natural rights thinking of the seventeenth century, but even then, if Haakonssen and Shapiro are in their differing ways at all correct, still evolving on into the eighteenth century when rights discourse began finally to escape its traditional subordination to the objective norms of natural law and to become identified with a "modern" version of moral conventionalism. But, however important philosophical considerations eventually became for natural rights thinking (and in the modern period they clearly did become very important), it should be acknowledged that its deepest roots reach down into the juristic, and especially the canonistic literature of the twelfth and thirteenth centuries.

IV

To that rather firm conclusion, perhaps I may be permitted to add a final, somewhat more tentative and diffident reflection. Much of what I have had to say has been directed, at least implicitly, at those whose scholarly interests lie in the modern period. In particular, it has been targeted on their regrettable (if understandable) reluctance to take more than fleeting account of the intricate and arcane claims and controversies prevalent among their medievalist colleagues. What follows, however, is properly directed to those of us who are medievalists, and it involves a word of caution. Impatient with the barriers to understanding posed by the traditional medieval-modern historiographic divide, all too conscious of the frequency with which alleged and much trumpeted novelties of the early modern period have well-developed root systems thrust deep into the patterns of medieval life and thought, and irritated, it may will be, by the bland willingness of many a blinkered modernist simply to ignore that fact, it could be all too easy for us, in turn, to commit our own historiographic sins. In saying that, what

I have in mind is the ease with which, in our eagerness to effect a perfectly warranted course correction, we could slip into claiming a bit too much for medieval antecedents, however important such antecedents may be, and, by so doing, miss the significant differences of emphasis and nuance that serve to distinguish modern and even early modern patterns of thinking from what had gone before. And here, I would suggest, a cautionary example may be found in the history of the development of notions of legitimation by consent, closely related, after all, as they came to be to natural law and natural rights discourse.[56]

Here, as is the case with the natural rights tradition, the medieval antecedents are clear, important, and often ignored. Here, too, those antecedents are to be found rooted in twelfth- and thirteenth-century juristic soil. Here notions of consent called into being by the practical exigencies of medieval political and ecclesiastical life were shaped by Romano-canonical corporational thinking, which transposed into the public constitutional sphere principles and procedures which, centuries earlier, the Roman lawyers had developed in the restricted realm of private law pertaining to property matters.[57] Here, again, ideas of juristic origin eventually connected with the older tradition of natural law thinking and were nudged thereby along a line of theoretical development more abstract and philosophical in nature and more universal in scope. And here, finally, via a complex process of development and transmission, a mode of thinking ultimately medieval in its provenance but mediated by the scholastic and political thinkers of the sixteenth century, survived to leave its imprint on the great social contract theorists of the seventeenth and eighteenth centuries.

But it must be insisted that it did not do so without undergoing in the post-medieval period a significant and crucial transposition. For what truly distinguishes the modern contractarian tradition of consent thinking running from Hobbes to Kant is the fact that, deploying the notion of a pre-political state of nature (not unknown, admittedly, to medieval authors but relocated now from periphery to center), it ascribes to the autonomous individual will "an importance... which never appeared before in the history of political philosophy." Despite the confusing ambiguities undoubtedly attaching to the notion of will, and despite the divergent conclusions contract theorists like Hobbes, Locke, and Rousseau drew from their stress on consent, this, it has well been urged, "provides a thread which holds the modern tradition together," "setting it off from the classical tradition"[58] and ultimately setting it off also, it should be added, even from the older tradition of consent theorizing that in one form or another had run from the late twelfth-century jurists down to the Protestant and Catholic political thinkers, constitutionalists, and resistance theorists of the sixteenth- and early-seventeenth centuries. Even for the most philosophically minded representatives of that older tradition (and despite some formulations arrestingly "modern" in their tonality), political consent appears most frequently to have meant the consent of communities, possessed at a minimum of the original right to choose their rulers, perhaps also to choose the form of government under which they were to live, maybe even to participate on some sort of continuing basis in the governmental process — those choices, however, "conditioned by the principle" that governmental authority as such was not ultimately the product of any free act of human willing but something, rather, that was "necessary and in some sense natural to man."[59]

The consent, however, that the seventeenth-century contract theorists and their successors had in mind was somewhat different in texture. It involved instead "a concatenation of voluntary individual acts," at base the assent of free and equal human beings existing in a pre-political state of nature but choosing now to enter political society and imposing on themselves, accordingly, an obligation which of their ultimate autonomy they could well avoid. And that transposition of the older tradition of consent thinking, while it clearly responds to Christian notions of moral autonomy and to an individualism and voluntarism that were ultimately of biblical derivation, appears to have occurred only in the wake of the Protestant Reformation, and then only after considerable delay, perhaps only, indeed, in the seventeenth century when the travail of religious and civil unrest had generated on the English religio-political scene and within one of the main branches of Protestantism an unambiguously sectarian impulse.[60]

If that was the case with the doctrine of consent, perhaps we should hesitate to brush to one side the stubborn conviction of so many modern commentators that there really *was* something novel about the particular type of discourse concerning the subjective natural rights of individuals that began to move to center stage in the political thinking of the seventeenth century.[61] That discourse appears to have carried with it the type of powerfully individualistic charge that its medieval forbears (*pace* de Lagarde and Villey) never quite possessed — a particularly strong form, if you wish, of Oakeshott's "idiom of individuality."[62] No dramatic breaks are evident, but already in the seventeenth century the process, it seems, had begun whereby the notion of individual rights gave rise to (or, at least, was connected to) the view that "morality is entirely the contingent product of the interactions of individuals," and whereby this notion of individual rights eventually escaped its lingering subordination to the objective moral constraints of natural law to become itself morally foundational, "the primary and basic moral feature of humanity."[63] And when in the eighteenth century that finally happened, the break with the medieval tradition of natural rights thinking was, of course, complete and a new modality of ethical thinking had definitively emerged.

EPILOGUE

Much of my effort in this book has been invested in the task of teasing apart the various strands that together make up the complex pattern of continuity and discontinuity characteristic of medieval and early modern natural law and natural rights discourse. And my mode of engagement with the issues involved has been, as indicated at the outset and in Whitehead's terms, scholarly-historical rather than speculative. At the same time it is my hope that that mode of engagement has not altogether concealed my admiring recognition of the contributions that those who have pursued something closer to Whitehead's speculative approach have made to our understanding of the history of natural law thinking. Here I have especially in mind not only the work of Whitehead himself but also that of philosophers like R. G. Collingwood, Michael Foster, and Michael Oakeshott.[1] If, even in their more "historical" moments, rather than proceeding in more earthbound historical fashion, these philosophers have often moved quasi-deductively to assert what in terms of the internal logic of ideas *must* have been the case, we should not miss the fact that their intuitions not infrequently turned out to have been, historically speaking, quite accurate, and their emphasis on the internal interconnections and affinities among ideas almost always illuminating. That emphasis usefully encourages a heightened sensitivity toward what Lovejoy called "the particular go" of ideas, the logical pressure they are capable of exerting on the minds of those that think them. It serves to draw attention also to the complex network of internal intellectual communications that, in probing the natural law tradition, we have seen linking together realms of discourse (theological, epistemological, scientific, moral, legal, political) that might otherwise have seemed quite disparate. In its absence, certainly, as those of us who aspire to be historians of political thought labor to plough what will often be very (if variously) demanding furrows, it would be all too easy for us to miss the pertinence to our efforts of Oakeshott's splendid intuition that there has probably been

> no theory of the nature of the world, of the activity of man, of the destiny of mankind, no theology or cosmology, perhaps even no metaphysics, that has not sought a reflection of itself in the mirror of political philosophy; certainly there has been no fully considered politics that has not looked for its reflection in eternity.[2]

That claim is surely not to be ignored. May we not, after all, insist that the age-old tradition of discourse and the several traditions of thought that together constitute the realm of natural law thinking together witness incontrovertibly to its wisdom?

NOTES

Preface

1. Arthur O. Lovejoy, "Reflections on the History of Ideas," *Journal of the History of Ideas* 1, no. 1 (1940): 3–23 (at 23).

2. For an assessment of this school, see Melvin Richter, "Opening a Dialogue and Recognizing an Achievement," *Archiv für Begriffsgeschichte* 39 (1996): 19–26. And for the debates about the notion of "influence," see Francis Oakley, "'Anxieties of Influence': Skinner, Figgis, Conciliarism and Early-Modern Constitutionalism,," *Past and Present* 151 (May 1996): 60–110.

1. Metaphysical Schemata and Intellectual Traditions

1. Michel Foucault, *Les mots et les choses* (Paris, 1966), trans. *The Order of Things* (New York, 1970). I draw the descriptive phrase quoted from Hayden White, "Foucault Decoded: Notes from the Underground," *History and Theory* 12 (1973): 23–54 (at 27).

2. Quentin Skinner, "Meaning and Understanding in the History of Ideas," *History and Theory* 8 (1969): 3–53 (at 39).

3. Lawrence Stone, *The Past and the Present* (Boston, 1981), 80–81, 83, 85–86.

4. For my own views on the matter, see Francis Oakley, *Omnipotence, Covenant, and Order: An Excursion in the History of Ideas from Abelard to Leibniz* (Ithaca and London, 1984), 15–40, and my *Politics and Eternity: Studies in the History of Medieval and Early-Modern Political Thought* (Leiden, Boston, and Cologne, 1999), 1–24, 333–41.

5. J. N. Figgis, *Political Thought from Gerson to Grotius: 1414–1625. Seven Studies* (New York, 1960), 60.

6. Jeremy Bentham, *Anarchical Fallacies*, art. 2, §1; in *Works*, ed. John Bowring, 11 vols. (London, 1843), 2:501.

7. David Hollinger, *Postethnic America: Beyond Multiculturalism* (New York, 1995), 9, 63, 65.

8. As Leo Strauss had pointed out in the 1950s, "Looking around us, we see two hostile camps, heavily fortified and strictly guarded. One is occupied by the liberals of various descriptions, the other by the Catholic and non-Catholic disciples of Thomas Aquinas" (*Natural Right and History* [Chicago, 1953], 7).

9. Robert P. George, ed., *Natural Law Theory: Contemporary Essays* (Oxford, 1992), v; David F. Forte, *Natural Law and Contemporary Public Policy* (Washington, D.C., 1998), ix; cf. 5. Not all those involved, however, in this episode of revival are altogether sanguine about the status and prospects of natural law theory. Thus Lloyd L. Weinreb: "... [A]lthough natural law has its adherents and periodically prompts a fierce attack from its detractors, the blunt truth is that philosophically it is a curiosity outside the mainstream, regarded mostly as a side-show and not to be taken seriously" ("The Moral Point of View," in *Natural Law, Liberalism and Morality: Contemporary Essays*, ed. Robert P. George [Oxford 1996], 195–212 [at 195]).

10. Paul E. Sigmund, *Natural Law in Political Thought* (Cambridge, MA, 1971), vii–viii.

11. See Robert P. George, ed., *Natural Law Theory*, vi–vii. Cf. Russell Hittinger, *A Critique of the New Natural Law Theory* (Notre Dame, IN, 1983), esp. 8, 190–96; Lloyd L. Weinreb, *Natural Law and Justice* (Cambridge, MA, 1987), 97–115; Ernest Fortin, "The New Natural Rights Theory and Natural Law," *Review of Politics* 44 (1982): 590–612.

12. Sigmund, *Natural Law in Political Thought*, vii. Similarly, A. P. d'Entrèves, *Natural Law: An Introduction to Legal Philosophy* (London, 1951), 10–11.

13. Hollinger, *Postethnic America*, 51–77.

14. Sir Ernest Barker, *Traditions of Civility* (Cambridge, 1948), 312–13; my attention is drawn to this passage by d'Entrèves, *Natural Law*, 8–9.

15. Thus Skinner, "Meaning and Understanding," 36 and 39.

16. For this distinction between "traditions of discourse" and "traditions of thought" I am indebted to Andrew Lockyer's thoughtful argument in his " 'Traditions' as Context in the History of Political Theory," *Political Studies* 27, no. 2 (1979): 201–17.

17. See d'Entrèves, *Natural Law*, 50.

18. Thus Raghuveer Singh, "John Locke and the Theory of Natural Law," *Political Studies* 9 (1961): 105–18 (at 105); Peter J. Stanlis, *Edmund Burke and the Natural Law* (Ann Arbor, MI, 1958), xiii, 13.

19. D'Entrèves, *Natural Law*, 49.

20. Strauss, *Natural Right and History*, 166.

21. See, for example, John Wild, *Plato's Modern Enemies and the Theory of Natural Law* (Chicago, 1953), 127–32; H. A. Rommen, "The Natural Law of the Renaissance Period," *Proceedings/Notre Dame, Natural Law Institute, 5 vols.* (Notre Dame, IN, 1949–53), 94–95; David Granfield, "The Scholastic Dispute on Justice: Aquinas versus Ockham," *Nomos VI: Justice*, ed. Carl Friedrich and John W. Chapman (New York, 1963), 240–42.

22. See, for example, R. I. Aaron, *John Locke* (Oxford, 1934), 267–68; Rommen, "The Natural Law of the Renaissance Period," 94–95; Granfield, "The Scholastic Dispute on Justice: Aquinas versus Ockham," *Nomos VI: Justice*, ed. Friedrich and Chapman, 240–42.

23. Antony Black, *Political Thought in Europe: 1250–1450* (Cambridge, 1992), 191. Cf. J. H. Burns in his introduction to *The Cambridge History of Political Thought 1450–1700*, ed. J. H. Burns and Mark Goldie (Cambridge, 1991), 1–3, and Brian Tierney, *Religion, Law, and the Growth of Constitutional Thought: 1150–1630* (Cambridge, 1982), 1.

24. Arthur O. Lovejoy and George Boas, *Primitivism and Related Ideas in Antiquity* (Baltimore, 1935), Appendix, 447–56.

25. *Digest* I, 1, §3: "Jus naturale est, quod natura omnia animalia docuit; nam jus istud non humani generis proprium, sed omnium animalium, qua in terra, quae in mari nascuntur, avium quoque commune est"; in P. Krueger, ed., *Corpus Juris Civilis*, 3 vols. (Berlin, 1894–1902), I, *Digesta*, 1.

26. Thus d'Entrèves, *Natural Law*, 7, 10–11; Sigmund, *Natural Law in Political Thought*, viii.

27. Peter Singer, *Animal Liberation: A New Ethics for Our Treatment of Animals* (New York, 1975); Tom Regan and Peter Singer, eds., *Animal Rights and Human Obligations* (Englewood Cliffs, N.J., 1976); Arnie Ness, "The Deep Ecological Movement: Some Philosophical Aspects," *Philosophical Inquiry* 8, nos. 1–2 (1986): 161–40; J. Baird Callicott, "Animal Liberation: A Triangular Affair," *Environmental Ethics* 2 (1980):

311–38. For a good, probing commentary on the arguments of both the animal liberationists and deep ecologists, see Luc Ferry, *The New Ecological Order,* trans. Carol Volk (Chicago and London, 1995).

28. A. N. Whitehead, *Adventures of Ideas* (New York: Mentor Books, 1958), 101–23. He lays out the distinction between natural law conceived of as immanent and imposed at 115–19 of this edition. M. Ginsberg, "The Concept of Juridical and Scientific Law," *Politica* 4 (March 1939): 1–15, makes an interesting attempt to apply Whitehead's distinction to the juridical sphere.

29. Whitehead, *Adventures of Ideas,* 116–17.

30. Ibid., 117–19, 126–27.

31. The reference here, of course, is to one of the four "necessary conditions" or "reasons for" any process which Aristotle described and which, since Cicero's day, have been known in the Western philosophical tradition as the "four causes." See Aristotle, *Physics,* ii, 3. 194b–195a; *Metaphysics,* v. 2. 1,013a–b. Cf. J. H. Randall, *Aristotle* (New York and London, 1962), 54, 65–7, 123–9. Randall (p. 126) helpfully describes the *Formal Cause* as responding to the question: "What is it?"; the *Material Cause* to the question: "Out of what is it made?"; the *Efficient Cause* to the question: "By what agent?"; and the *Final Cause* to the question: "For what end?" And he illustrates the four causes as follows: "Thus we can ask, What is it? It is a flag. Out of what is it made? Bunting. By what was it made? The firm of Rosenkranz and Guildenstern. For what was it made? To serve as a patriotic symbol."

32. Cited from Michael Bertram Crowe, *The Changing Profile of Natural Law* (The Hague, 1977), 32–33.

33. For a helpful survey of the range of interpretative approaches to Hobbes, see W. H. Greenleaf, "Hobbes: The Problem of Interpretation," *Hobbes-Forschungen,* ed. Reinhart Koselleck and Roman Schnur (Berlin, 1969), 9–31. See, more recently, A. P. Martinich, *The Two Gods of Leviathan: Thomas Hobbes on Religion and Politics* (Cambridge, 1992).

34. Michael Oakeshott, ed., *The Leviathan of Thomas Hobbes* (Oxford, 1946), Introduction, xx–xxi, xxvi–ix, xlvi, lii–lv.

35. *Timaeus* 83E contains the phrase sometimes translated (e.g., by Jowett) as "in violation of the laws of nature." F. M. Cornford, *Plato's Cosmology* (London, 1937), 339, dismisses this as "a mistranslation," renders it instead as "contrary to the established use of nature," and

adds "all that is meant is the customary and normal process by which blood is healthily formed."

36. See Cornford, *Plato's Cosmology*, 37–39.

2. Laws of Nature: The Scientific Concept

1. Joseph Needham, "Human Law and the Laws of Nature," in Joseph Needham, *The Grand Titration: Science and Society in East and West* (Toronto, 1969), 299–333 (at 308).

2. Thus J. E. McGuire, "Boyle's Conception of Nature," *Journal of the History of Ideas* 33 (1972): 523–42 (at 524).

3. Robert Boyle, *The Christian Virtuoso*, in *The Works of the Honourable Robert Boyle*, ed. Thomas Birch, new ed., 6 vols. (London, 1972), 5:521; *A Free Inquiry*, in ibid., 170–71.

4. Francisco Suarez, *De Legibus ac Deo Legislatore*, lib. I, cap. 1, and lib. II, cap. 2, in *Selections from Three Works of Francisco Suárez, S.J.*, 2 vols. (Oxford, 1944), 1:8 and 104. Also his *Metaphysicarum Disputationum*, 2 vols., disp. XXII, sect. 4, XXX, sect. 17 (Mainz, 1605), 1:568–69 and 2:150.

5. Needham, *The Grand Titration*, 330. Cf. Joseph Needham and Wang Ling, *Science and Civilization in China* (Cambridge, 1956), 2:582–83.

6. The term has of late been brought into question. See, e.g., Steven Shapin, *The Scientific Revolution* (Chicago and London, 1996), 1–4.

7. R. G. Collingwood, *The Idea of Nature* (Oxford, 1945), 1–9.

8. Francis Oakley, "Christian Theology and the Newtonian Science: The Rise of the Concept of the Laws of Nature," *Church History* 30 (1961): 433–57; John R. Milton, "The Origin and Development of the Concept of the 'Laws of Nature,'" *Archives européennes de Sociologie* 22 (1981): 173–95; Matthias Schramm, "Roger Bacons Begriff vom Naturgesetz," in *Die Renaissance der Wissenschaften im 12. Jahrhundert*, ed. Peter Weimar (Zürich, 1981), 197–209; Jane E. Ruby, "The Origins of Scientific 'Law,'" *Journal of the History of Ideas* 47, no. 3 (1986): 341–59.

9. Thus the scholastic authors Peter of Spain, William of Shyreswood, and Roger Bacon referred to the fundamental logical principle of

noncontradiction as the *lex contradictionis*. See Ruby, "The Origins of Scientific 'Law,'" 348–49.

10. Alistair Crombie, *Medieval and Early Modern Science* (New York, 1959), II, 14; cf. Ruby, "The Origins of Scientific 'Law,'" 343–4; Schramm, "Roger Bacons Begriff vom Naturgesetz," 203–4.

11. Crombie, *Medieval and Early Modern Science*, II, 24.

12. Needham, *The Grand Titration*, 310.

13. See Ruby, "The Origins of Scientific 'Law,'" 350–59.

14. Ibid., 342–47.

15. Descartes, Letters to Mersenne, April 15 and May 27, 1630, in *Oeuvres de Descartes*, ed. Charles Adam and Paul Tannery, 11 vols. (Paris, 1964–74), 1:145, 151–52; also his *Meditationes de prima philosophia*, Resp. ad sextas objectiones, ibid., 7:436. Cf. his Letter to Mesland, May 2, 1644, in ibid., 4:118–19.

16. *Essay Concerning Human Understanding*, IV, iii, §§28–29, ed. Peter H. Nidditch (Oxford, 1975), 559–60.

17. Boyle, *The Christian Virtuoso*, in *Works*, ed. Birch, V, 521.

18. Sir Isaac Newton, *Philosophiae Naturalis Principia Mathematica*, in *Opera quae exstant omnia*, ed. Samuel Horsley, 5 vols. (London, 1782), 2: xx and xxiii; the translation cited is that by Andrew Motte, revised by Florian Cajori (Berkeley, 1946), xxvii and xxxii; Newton, *Principia Mathematica: Scholium Generale*, in *Opera*, ed. Horsley, 3:170–74; trans. Motte and Cajori, 542.

19. Newton, *Principia Mathematica*, Praefatio; ibid., Axiomata, Lex I; ibid., Lib. III, Scholium Generale; trans. Motte and Cajori, xvii, 13, 543–47; *Opticks*; in (respectively), *Opera*, ed. Horsley, 2:ix, III, 174, IV, 263.

20. Edgar Zilsel, "The Genesis of the Concept of Physical Law," *Philosophical Review* 51 (1942): 245–79 (at 277–79).

21. Needham, *Science and Civilization in China*, 2:542. Derk Bodde, however, insists that "in addition to the dominant viewpoint...argued for by Dr. Needham, a minority viewpoint also exists, expressed by a very few early Chinese thinkers, which was a good deal more congenial to the ideas underlying the 'laws of nature' than would initially be expected" (*Chinese Thought, Society, and Science: The Intellectual and Social Background of Science and Technology in pre-modern China* [Honolulu, 1991], 344).

22. Needham, *Science and Civilization in China*, 2:543.

23. Francis Oakley, *Omnipotence, Covenant, and Order: An Excursion in the History of Ideas from Abelard to Leibniz* (Ithaca and London, 1984), 93–118; idem, *Politics and Eternity: Studies in the History of Medieval and Early-Modern Political Thought* (Leiden, Boston, and Cologne, 1999), 318–27.

24. E.g., *Confessions*, VII, 9, 20, 21.

25. For a discussion of this point and its implications, see the essays gathered together in Daniel O'Connor and Francis Oakley, eds., *Creation: the Impact of an Idea* (New York, 1969).

26. *Job* 38:14, 12, 31, 40:2. Cf. Thomas Hobbes, *Leviathan*, Part II, ch. 31; ed. Michael Oakeshott (Oxford, 1946), 234–35.

27. Boyle, *A Free Inquiry*, in *Works*, ed. Birch, 5:163–64, where, having cited the Aristotelian denial to God of both the creation and the providential governance of the world, he confessed that he took "divers of Aristotle's opinions relating to religion to be more unfriendly, not to say pernicious, than those of several other heathen philosophers."

28. Thomas Aquinas, *Summa theologiae*, Ia IIae, qu. 91, art. 1 and 2; qu. 93, art. 1.

29. For the complexities involved in the ongoing attempt to classify the various tendencies traditionally lumped under the rather capacious umbrella of late-medieval nominalism, see Heiko A. Oberman, "Some Notes on the Theology of Nominalism," *Harvard Theological Review* 53 (1960): 47–76; William J. Courtenay, "Nominalism and Late Medieval Religion," in Charles Trinkaus and Heiko Oberman, eds. *The Pursuit of Holiness in Late Medieval and Renaissance Religion* (Leiden, 1974), 26–59; idem, "Current Theology: Nominalism and Late Medieval Thought, A Bibliographical Essay," *Theological Studies* 33 (1972): 716–34.

30. The pertinent texts of Ockham are analyzed in Lucan Freppert, *The Basis of Morality according to William of Ockham* (Chicago, 1988), 97–101.

31. Pierre d'Ailly, *Quaestiones Super I, III et IV Sententiarum* (Lyons, 1500), I, qu. 6, art. 2, L, f. 97r.

32. See Kevin McDonnell, "Does William of Ockham Have a Theory of Natural Law?" *Franciscan Studies* 34 (1974): 383–92 (see esp. 386–87).

33. Thus David C. Lindberg, *The Beginning of Western Science* (Chicago and London, 1992), 242–43.

34. Ibid.

35. Edward Grant, *The Foundations of Modern Science in the Middle Ages* (Cambridge, 1996), 74.

36. Robert Holcot, *Super libros Sapientiae* (Hagenau, 1494), lect. 145B. I cite the translation in Heiko A. Oberman, ed., *Forerunners of the Reformation: The Shape of Late Medieval Thought* (New York, 1966), 149. For the covenantal theme in late medieval theology in general, see Berndt Hamm, *Promissio, Pactum, Ordinatio: Freiheit und Selbstbindung Gottes in der scholastischen Gnadenlehre* (Tübingen, 1977).

37. On which, see the brief statements in Oakley, *Politics and Eternity*, 286–87.

38. Oakley, *Politics and Eternity*, 287–88; William J. Courtenay, *Capacity and Volition: A History of the Distinction of Absolute and Ordained Power* (Bergamo, 1990).

39. Oakley, *Politics and Eternity*, 288–91, and the works of Oakley, Gijsbert van den Brink, Marilyn Adams, Eugenio Randi, Katherine H. Tachau, Heiko A. Oberman, and Leonard A. Kennedy referred to therein.

40. Oakley, *Politics and Eternity*, 304–5.

41. Ibid., 292–318; B. J. T. Dobbs, *The Janus Faces of Genius: The Role of Alchemy in Newton's Thought* (Cambridge, 1991), 110–13, and the pertinent works she cites in nn. 45 and 46; James E. Force, "Newton's God of Dominion," in James E. Force and Richard H. Popkin, *Essays on the Context, Nature and Influence of Newton's Theology* (Dordrecht, 1990), 75–102; J. E. McGuire, *Tradition and Innovation: Newton's Metaphysics of Nature* (Dordrecht, Boston, and London, 1995), 214–27.

42. Descartes to Mersenne, April 15, 1630, in *Oeuvres de Descartes*, ed. Adam and Tannery, 1:145.

43. Pierre Gassendi, *Disquisitio metaphysica seu dubitationes et instantiae adversus Renatus Cartesii metaphysicam et responsa*, ed. and trans. Bernard Rochat (Paris, 1962), 481. I reproduce Margaret Osler's translation of this passage in *Divine Will and the Mechanical Philosophy: Gassendi and Descartes on Contingency and Necessity in the Created World* (Cambridge, 1994), 1; cf. 153–65.

44. Walter Charleton, *The Darkness of Atheism Dispelled by the Light of Nature: A Physico-Theologicall Treatise* (London, 1652), 329.

45. *Principia mathematica*, in *Opera*, ed. Horsley, 2:xx and xxiii; trans. Motte and Cajori, xxvii and xxxii.

46. See Francis Oakley, "Christian Virtuoso and Scholastic Tradition: Robert Boyle and the *potentia dei absoluta et ordinata*," in *The Work of Heiko A. Oberman: Papers from the Symposium on His Seventieth Birthday*, ed. Thomas A. Brady, Jr., Katherine G. Brady, Susan Karant-Nunn, James D. Tracy (Leiden and Boston, 2003), 163–87 (at 183–86), where full references to the pertinent texts may be found.

47. William of Ockham, *Scriptum in librum primum Sententiarum* (*Ordinatio*), Prol. qu. VII; ed. G. Gál and S. Brown (New York, 1967), 197, 202; idem, *Quodl.* VI, qu. 1, 2 and 4, in *Quodlibeta septem*, ed. J. C. Wey (New York, 1980), 585–86, 588, 591, 598.

48. D'Ailly, *Sent.* IV, qu. 1, art. 1, N. fol. 188r; *Tractatus de legibus et sectis*, in Jean Gerson, *Opera omnia*, ed. Louis Ellies Dupin, 5 vols. (Antwerp, 1706), 1:793

49. Thus, e.g., Bodde, *Chinese Thought, Society, and Science*, 344, where he observes that "...the relative weakness of the idea of a truly all-powerful deity, is a probable major reason why the concept of 'laws of nature' developed no further in China than it did."

3. Natural Law: Disputed Moments of Transition

1. Samuel Pufendorf, *De jure naturae et gentium. Libri Octo*, Lib. II, cap. 3, §19; trans. C. H. and W. A. Oldfather, 2 vols. (Oxford, 1934), II, 215.

2. Hugo Grotius, *De jure belli et pacis*. Prolegomena, §§6, 9, 11; trans. Francis W. Kelsey et al., 2 vols. (Oxford, 1925), 2:11, 13.

3. Ibid., Prol. 11; 2:13.

4. Thus Jean Barbeyrac, cited from Brian Tierney, *The Idea of Natural Rights: Studies on Natural Rights, Natural Law and Church Law 1150–1625* (Atlanta, 1997), 318.

5. Thus Knud Haakonssen, "From Natural Law to the Rights of Man: A European Perspective on American Debates," in *A Culture of Rights: The Bill of Rights in Philosophy, Politics, and Law*, ed. M. J. Lacey and K. Haakonssen (Cambridge, 1991), 19–51 (at 25).

6. Thus, e.g., A. P. d'Entrèves, *Natural Law: An Introduction to Legal Philosophy* (London, 1951), 51–54; M. B. Crowe, *The Changing Profile of Natural Law* (The Hague, 1977), 221–28; Richard Tuck, *Natural Rights Theories: Their origin and development* (Cambridge, 1979), 58–81; idem, *Philosophy and Government, 1572–1651* (Cambridge, 1993), xiv–xv; Knud Haakonssen, *Natural Law and Moral Philosophy from Grotius to the Scottish Enlightenment* (Cambridge, 1996), 26–30.

7. George H. Sabine, *A History of Political Theory* (New York, 1938), 420–25.

8. Thus d'Entrèves, *Natural Law,* 51: "It is not in its content that Grotius' theory of natural law breaks away from Scholasticism. It is in its methods, . . . " framed, in effect, on the analogy of mathematics. More recently, puzzling over the fact that Grotius's contemporaries and successors so often saw him as a great innovator, Brian Tierney has portrayed him as a bridge figure, "deploying old arguments, not only in a new idiom, but also in a changed context where they took on new meanings and found a new significance." If he "did not create a new theory of natural rights and natural law . . . what he did achieve was equally important. He made it possible for the old theory to live on in the modern world" (*The Idea of Natural Rights,* 316–42 [at 339, 342]). For a robust rejection of the traditional claim that Grotius was responsible for founding "a new and distinctive theory of natural law," as well as an expressed degree of skepticism about the very existence of any such "modern school," see Johan P. Sommerville, "Selden, Grotius, and the Seventeenth-Century Intellectual Revolution in Moral and Political Theory," in *Rhetoric and Law in Early Modern Europe,* ed. Victoria Kahn and Lorna Hutson (New Haven and London, 2001), 318–44.

9. Leonard Besselink, "The Impious Hypothesis Revisited," *Grotiana* 9 (1988): 3–63 (at 62).

10. A. H. Chroust, "Hugo Grotius and the Scholastic Natural Law Tradition," *The New Scholasticism* 17 (1943): 101–33; J. St. Leger, *The "Etiamsi daremus" of Hugo Grotius: A Study in the Origins of International Law* (Rome, 1962), esp. 45–57, 122–34; P. Haggenmacher, *Grotius et la doctrine de la guerre juste* (Paris, 1983), 479–523; Besselink.

11. Hugo Grotius, *De jure praedae commentarius: Commentary on the Law of Prize and Booty,* trans. Gwladys L. Williams and Walter H. Zandel from the Original Manuscript of 1604 (New York and London,

1964). Prolegomena, cap. II, Rule 1: "*What God has shown to be His Will, that is law.* This axiom points directly to the cause of law, and is rightly laid down as a primary principle" (p. 8). A little later on the same page he at least entertains the possible rectitude of the view that "a given thing is just because God wills it, rather than that God wills the thing because it is just." And he notes that "the Will of God is revealed, not only through oracles and supernatural portents, but above all in the very design of the Creator; for it is from this last source that the law of nature is derived." Also cap. III [p. 35]: "For just as the Will of God — constituting the notion of justice . . . is revealed to us through nature, so also is it revealed through the Scriptures." Cf. St. Leger, *The "Etiamsi Daremus" of Hugo Grotius*, 137–42; Haggenmacher, *Grotius et la doctrine de la guerre juste*, 468–70, 517–21. I am unconvinced by Besselink's somewhat convoluted attempt to deny the voluntarist character of Grotius's position in the *De jure praedae* ("The Impious Hypothesis Revisited," 47–54). It would appear to be predicated on a very rigid construction of what he labels as "strict voluntarism."

12. Grotius, *De jure belli et pacis*, Prolegomena, §12; I, cap. 1, §x, 2. Trans. Kelsey, 2:14 and 39.

13. Ibid., I, cap. 1, x, 1–2, 5 (pp. 38–40). At the same time (Prol. 12 [p. 14]), and to complicate the picture somewhat, Grotius affirmed that the natural law is nonetheless rightly attributed to God because it is he who implanted in man those "essential traits" from which it proceeds.

14. Elsewhere (in his *De imperio*) Grotius adds a further nuance by distinguishing (somewhat reluctantly, it seems) between God's power as absolute and as ordained. Thus, in effect, he conceded that of his absolute power God had been free not to create man, but insisted, nonetheless, that *de potentia ordinata* God had chosen to endow man with "a nature using reason and being eminently sociable," and, as a result, had necessarily to approve "actions in harmony with that nature." For this point, see Besselink, "The Impious Hypothesis Revisited," 38–39, and for the *potentia dei absoluta et ordinata* distinction, see above, chapter 2, 55–60, and below, 79–80, 81–86.

15. Though, as Besselink rightly insists, from that it does not follow that Grotius was actually *influenced* by Suarez, as has often been alleged. See "The Impious Hypothesis Revisited," 59–62.

16. Two good accounts of this ongoing debate and assessments of its historical importance may be found in Haakonssen, *Natural Law and Moral Philosophy*, and T. J. Hochstrasser, *Natural Law Theories in the Early Enlightenment* (Cambridge, 2000).

17. Plato, *Euthyphro*, §§7A, 9E, 10E–11A; the Greek text with an English translation by Henry North Fowler (Cambridge, MA, 1932), 22–23, 34–35, 38–41.

18. Gottfried Wilhelm Leibniz, "Meditation on the Common Concept of Justice" (ca. 1702–3), in Leibniz, *Political Writings*, ed. and trans. Patrick Riley, 2nd ed. (Cambridge, 1988), 45–46.

19. Leibniz, *Monadology*, prop. 46; cited from G. W. Leibniz, *Philosophical Writings*, ed. G. H. R. Parkinson (London, 1973), 186. Cf. Leibniz, "Opinions on the Principles of Pufendorf" (1706), in Leibniz, *Political Writings*, trans. and ed. Riley, 71–72: "... [J]ustice follows certain rules of equality and of proportion [which are] no less founded in the immutable nature of things, and in the divine ideas, than are the principles of arithmetic and of geometry. So that no one will maintain that justice and goodness originate in the divine will: an unheard of paradox by which Descartes showed how great can be the errors of great men." I follow here the excellent discussion of the issue by Hochstrasser, *Natural Law Theories in the Early Enlightenment*, 72–89. Cf. Haakonssen, *Natural Law and Moral Philosophy*, 46–91.

20. G. W. Leibniz, *Monadology*, props. 83 and 84; in Leibniz, *Philosophical Writings*, ed. Parkinson, 192–93; idem, "Preliminary Dissertation on the Conformity of Faith with Reason," in G. W. Leibniz, *Theodicy: Essays on the Goodness of God, the Freedom of Man, and the Origin of Evil*, ed. A. Farrer (New Haven, 1952), 94.

21. Citing here the account of Hochstrasser, *Natural Law Theories in the Early Enlightenment*, 159–70 (at 164–65).

22. Francisco Suarez, *De Legibus ac Deo Legislatore*, Lib. II, cap. 6, §4; in James Brown Scott, ed., *Selections from Three Works of Francisco Suarez, S.J.*, 2 vols. (Oxford, 1944), 1:121 (Latin); 2:190 (English).

23. Ralph Cudworth, *Treatise Concerning Immutable Morality*, Bk. I, chs. 1 and 3; in Cudworth, *The True Intellectual System of the Universe*, ed. Thomas Baird, 2 vols. (New York, 1938), 2, esp. 369–71.

24. *Summa theologiae* (*ST*), 1a 2ae, qu. 90, art. 1 *resp.*; qu. 91, art. 1 and *resp.*; qu. 93, art. 1.

25. *ST,* 1a 2ae, qu. 91, art. 2.

26. *ST,* 1a 2ae, qu. 91, art. 4. Cf. Grotius's "divine volitional law."

27. *ST,* 1a 2ae, qu. 91, art. 3; qu. 95, art. 1.

28. *ST,* 1a 2ae, qu. 90, art. 4, *resp.;* qu. 93, art. 3; qu. 95, art. 2.

29. A good sense of the current state of play in Ockham studies can be garnered from the essays gathered together in *The Cambridge Companion to Ockham,* ed. Paul Vincent Spade (Cambridge, 1999), esp. chapters 10–13, 227–325 (by Peter King, Marilyn McCord Adams, A. S. McGrade, and John Kilcullen, respectively) which deal with his ethical thinking, doctrine of natural law, and political writings. See also David W. Clark, "Voluntarism and Rationalism in the Ethics of Ockham," *Franciscan Studies* 31 (1971): 72–87; Kevin McDonnell, "Does William of Ockham Have a Theory of Natural Law?" ibid., 34 (1974): 383–92; Marilyn McCord Adams, "The Structures of Ockham's Moral Theory," ibid., 46 (1986): 1–35; Lucan Freppert, *The Basis of Morality according to William of Ockham* (Chicago, 1988).

30. Thus Heinrich Rommen, *The Natural Law* (St. Louis, 1947), 58–59. Cf. John Wild, *Plato's Modern Enemies and the Theory of Natural Law* (Chicago, 1953), 66, 132; Paul Helm, ed., *Divine Command and Morality* (Oxford, 1981), Introduction, 3; McDonnell, "Does William of Ockham Have a Theory of Natural Law?" 383–92.

31. Thus J. B. Morrall, "Some Notes on a Recent Interpretation of William of Ockham's Political Philosophy," *Franciscan Studies* 9 (1949): 335–69 (criticizing Georges de Lagarde); Philotheus Boehner, "Ockham's Political Ideas," *Review of Politics* 3 (1943): 465–66; Max A. Shephard, "William of Ockham and the Higher Law," *American Political Science Review* 26 (1932): 1005–23 (at 1009), and 27 (1933): 24–38. Cf. George H. Sabine, *A History of Political Theory* (New York, 1955), 306.

32. See the eminently clear discussion of this contrast in McDonnell, "Does William of Ockham Have a theory of Natural Law?" 383–92.

33. See *Dialogus* I, VI, cap. 100; in Melchior Goldast, ed., *Monarchia Sancti Romani Imperii,* 3 vols. (Frankfurt, 1668), 2:629, lines 45–46.

34. *Dial.* III, II, i, cap. 10, ibid., III, II, iii, cap. 6, in Goldast, 2:878, lines 27–31, 932, line 65, 933, line 1; "... quia jus naturale est

immutabile primo modo et invariabile ac indispensabile." This latter reference is to the first of the three "modes" of natural which Ockham describes as that "quod est conforme ratione naturali, quae in nullo casu fallit, sicut est 'non maechaberis', 'non mentieris' et hujusnodi." The version of this crucial chapter printed in Goldast is marred by serious textual corruptions. A new and accurate version based on the manuscripts may be found in H. S. Offler, "The Three Modes of Natural Law in Ockham: A Revision of the Text," *Franciscan Studies* 37 (1977): 207–18.

35. Citing here Clark, "Voluntarism and Rationalism in the Ethics of Ockham," 77.

36. William of Ockham, *Quaestiones in librum secundum Sententiarum (Reportatio)*, II, qu. 15; ed. Gedeon Gál and Rega Wood (New York, 1981), 352.

37. *Reportatio*, II, qu. 3–4; ed. Gál and Wood, 59.

38. Ibid.

39. Thus Frederick Copleston, *A History of Philosophy*, 7 vols. (Garden City, N.Y., 1962–65), 3, Part 1, 118–22.

40. For such claims by Morrall, Boehner, and Shephard, see above n. 31; similarly, more recently, Brian Tierney, *The Idea of Natural Rights: Studies on Natural Rights, Natural Law and Church Law 1150–1625* (Atlanta, 1997), 9, 98–100, where he evokes the authority also of W. Kölmel, *Wilhelm von Ockham und sein Kirchenpolitischen Schriften* (Essen, 1962).

41. Boehner, "Ockham's Political Ideas," 465–66.

42. Georges de Lagarde, *La naissance de l'esprit laïque au déclin du moyen age*, new ed., 5 vols. (Louvain and Paris, 1956–63), 5:289; Boehner art. cit.

43. McDonnell, "Does William of Ockham Have a theory of Natural Law?" 384–85.

44. William of Ockham, *Quaestiones variae*, qu. VII, art. 4; ed. G. I. Etzkorn, F. E. Kelley and J. C. Wey (New York, 1984), 395.

45. Freppert, *The Basis of Morality According to William of Ockham*, 83, n. 1.

46. William of Ockham, *Scriptum in librum primum Sententiarum (Ordinatio)*, dist. 41, qu. unica; ed. G. I. Etzkorn and F. E. Kelley (New York, 1979), 610.

47. Ockham, *Dial.* III, II, iii, cap. 6, in Goldast, 2:934, lines 1–9.

48. A. S. McGrade, "Natural Law and Moral Omnipotence," in Spade, ed., *The Cambridge Companion to Ockham,* 282. Cf. idem., *The Political Thought of William of Ockham: Personal and Institutional Principles* (Cambridge, 1974), 165, referring to Ockham's discussion of the exception to the precepts of natural law which God made when he ordered Abraham to sacrifice Isaac.

49. McGrade, "Natural Law and Moral Omnipotence," in Spade, ed., *The Cambridge Companion to Ockham,* 276–78 and n. 1. McGrade bases this claim partly on *Dial.* III, II, iii, cap. 6, 934, lines 3–9 ("Every law that is from God, who is the creator [*conditor*] of nature, can be called a divine law; but every natural law is from God, who is the creator of nature; therefore" etc.). But he also advances the claim "mainly as a friendly supplement to what Ockham says." A similar point of view is advanced by Freppert, *The Basis of Morality according to William of Ockham,* 178–79, who asks: "...[F]rom the aspect of God's ordered power, can we not also speak of a 'natural revelation' made from God to man?" adding: "From its knowledge of created things the human mind 'begins its journey' to the mind of God," and concluding that "the principles and precepts discovered by human reason in the natural order are the natural, non-positive, commands of God."

50. See above, chapter 2, 55–60.

51. William of Ockham, *Quaestiones in librum secundum Sententiarum (Reportatio),* qu. 15; ed. Gál and Wood, 352–53; *Quodlibet VI,* qu. 1, in William of Ockham, *Quodlibeta septem,* ed. J. C. Wey (New York, 1980), 585–87; *Opus nonaginta dierum,* cap. 95, in R. F. Bennett and H. S. Offler, eds., *Guillelmi de Ockham: Opera politica,* 3 vols. (Manchester, 1940–56), 2:715–29; *Tractatus contra Benedictum,* Lib. III, cap. 3, ed. Offler, *Guillelmi de Ockham: Opera politica,* 3:230–34. Cf. *Dial.* I, V, ii, in Goldast, 2:470, lines 13–19.

52. William of Ockham, *Quaestiones variae,* qu. VII, art. 4; ed. Etzkorn, Kelley and Wey, 393–94.

53. He had also identified in similar terms the fifteenth-century scholastic. Andreas de Novocastro, who, while committing himself to an ethical voluntarism aligned with Ockham and d'Ailly, did not develop any fully fledged doctrine of natural law. For a useful brief discussion,

see Leonard A. Kennedy, "Andrew of Novo Castro, O.F.M. and the Moral Law," *Franciscan Studies* 48 (1988): 28–39.

54. Pierre d'Ailly, *Quaestiones super I, III et IV Sententiarum* (Nicolaus Wolff: Lyons, 1500), *Princ. in II Sent.*, P, fol. 31 v.

55. D'Ailly, *Sent.* IV, qu. 1, art. 1, E, fol. 185r; ibid., F, fol. 185 v.

56. D'Ailly, *Princ. in I Sent.*, K, f. 23v; *Sent.* I, qu. 3, art. 1, M, fol. 72 v.

57. D'Ailly, *Princ. in I Sent.*, K. fol. 23v.

58. D'Ailly, *Princ. In I Sent.*, H, fol. 22v; *Sent.* I, qu. 14, art. 3, T-V, fol., 174v.

59. For Essay VII, see John Locke, *Essays on the Law of Nature*, ed. and trans. W. Von Leyden (Oxford, 1954), 190–203. For an "intellectualist" reading of this text, see Raghuveer Singh, "John Locke and the Theory of Natural Law," *Political Studies* 9 (1961): 105–18 (at 112).

60. See Richard J. Aaron, *John Locke*, 2nd. ed. (Oxford, 1955), 8–14, who concludes that if Locke "is to be grouped with any European group we must follow Leibniz in grouping him with the Gassendists." Cf. Thomas M. Lennan, "The Epicurean New Way of Ideas: Gassendi, Locke, and Berkeley," in *Atoms, pneuma, and tranquility: Epicurean and Stoic themes in European Thought*, ed. Margaret J. Osler (Cambridge, 1991), 259–71.

61. Thus G. A. J. Rogers, "Locke, Law and the Laws of Nature," in *John Locke: Symposium Wolfenbuttel 1979*, ed. Reinhardt Brandt (Berlin and New York, 1981), 146–62 (at 154–56, 147), where he adds: "…only through an awareness of the interactions between epistemological, moral and theological viewpoints can we approach a proper understanding" of what he has to say about natural law. Cf. Michael Ayers, *Locke*, 2 vols. (London and New York, 1991), 2:131–32.

62. *Essay Concerning Human Understanding*, IV, iii, §§28–29, ed. Peter H. Nidditch (Oxford, 1975), 559–60. Cf. John R. Milton, "John Locke and the Nominalist Tradition," in Brandt, 127–45 (at 135–41); Ayers, *Locke*, 2:150–53; Rogers, "Locke, Law and the Laws of Nature," 153.

63. Ayers, *Locke*, 2:189–90: "The necessity of the law is hypothetical but hard: God was free to will what laws he liked in that he was free to create what things he liked, but in creating free and rational beings capable of pleasure and pain he ipso facto willed a certain law for those

beings; just as, in choosing to create matter, he chose certain necessary laws of motion."

64. Essay VII in Von Leyden, ed., *Essays on the Law of Nature*, 192–93, 198–99.

65. Ibid., 198–201 (italics mine).

66. See Locke's *Journal*, entry for July 9, 1676, Ms. Locke, fol. 1, 313–4, printed in Von Leyden, *Essays on the Law of Nature*, 259. Similarly, the entry under Sunday, September 18, 1681, printed in Lord King, *The Life of John Locke*, new ed., 2 vols. (London, 1830), 2:232–34, where he is discussing miracles.

67. *First Treatise of Government*, §6; *Second Treatise*, §195; ed. Peter Laslett, *John Locke: Two Treatises of Government* (Cambridge, 1988), 144, 395–96.

4. Natural Rights: Origins and Grounding

1. Kenneth Minogue, "The History of the Idea of Human Rights," in Walter Laqueur and Barry Rubin, eds., *The Human Rights Reader* (Philadelphia, 1979), 3–16 (at 3).

2. For the dimensions of the body of literature involved, see Rex Martin and James W. Nickel, "A Bibliography on the Nature and Foundations of Rights, 1942–1977," *Political Theory* 6, no. 6 (1978): 395–413, and idem, "Recent Work on the Concept of Rights," *American Philosophical Quarterly* 17 (1980): 165–80. For works of an historical nature, see Richard Tuck, *Natural Rights Theories: Their origin and development* (Cambridge, 1979); Brian Tierney, *The Idea of Natural Rights: Studies on Natural Rights, Natural Law and Church Law 1150–1625* (Atlanta, 1997), 349–67.

3. Thomas Hobbes, *Leviathan*, I, 14; ed. Michael Oakeshott (Oxford, 1946), 84.

4. Thus Annabel S. Brett, *Liberty, Right and Nature: Individual rights in later scholastic thought* (Cambridge, 1997), 2.

5. Wesley N. Hohfeld, *Fundamental Legal Conceptions* (New Haven, 1919), esp. 35–64. Cf. John Finnis, *Natural law and Natural Rights* (Oxford, 1980), 199–205.

6. Charles J. Reid Jr., "The Canonistic Contribution to the Western Rights Tradition: An Historical Inquiry," *Boston College Law Review* 33 (1991/1992): 37–92 (at 91). Cf. Brett, *Liberty, Right and Nature*, 2–6.

7. A good sense of the current state of play can be gleaned from Tierney, *The Idea of Natural Rights*, and from his "Natural Law and Natural Rights: Old Problems and Recent Approaches" (with responses by John Finnis, Douglas Kries, and Michael P. Zuckert), *Review of Politics* 64, no. 3 (2002): 389–420.

8. Leo Strauss, *Natural Right and History* (Chicago, 1953); C. B. Macpherson, *The Political Theory of Possessive Individualism: Hobbes to Locke* (Oxford, 1962). And for a latter-day Straussian view, Ernest L. Fortin, "On the Presumed Medieval Origin of Individual Rights," in Ernest L. Fortin, *Classical Christianity and the Political Order: Reflections on the Theologico-Political Problem*, ed. J. Brian Benestad (New York and London, 1996), 243–64. Cf. Robert J. Kraynack, *Christian Faith and Modern Democracy: God and Politics in the Fallen World* (Notre Dame, IN, 2001), 110–13.

9. Tuck, *Natural Rights Theories*, 25. While acknowledging earlier moves in that direction, he asserts that "...it was Jean Gerson, who really created the theory"; Georges de Lagarde, *La Naissance de l'esprit laïque au déclin du moyen âge*, first edition, 6 vols. (Paris, 1934–46), 6; second edition, 5 vols. (Paris, 1956–70), 5; Michel Villey, "La genèse du droit subjectif chez Guillaume d'Occam," *Archives de philosophie du droit* 9 (1964): 94–127; Michel Bastit, *Naissance de la loi moderne: La pensée de la loi de saint Thomas à Suarez* (Paris, 1990). Cf. Louis Dumont, *Essays on Individualism: Modern Ideology in Anthropological Perspective* (Chicago, 1993), 62–66; John Finnis, *Aquinas: Moral, Political, and Legal Theory* (Oxford, 1998), esp. 170–76; Tierney, *The Idea of Natural Rights*; Reid, "The Canonistic Contribution to the Western Rights Tradition."

10. Tierney, *The Idea of Natural Rights*, 1. Cf. the pertinent discussion in Jack Donnelly, *Universal Human Rights in Theory and Practice*, 2nd ed. (Ithaca and London, 2003), 57–70.

11. See, for example, in addition to the works of Strauss, Macpherson, Fortin, and Minogue already cited, such works as A. P. d'Entrèves, *Natural Law: An Introduction to Legal Philosophy* (London, 1951), 48–63; Norbert Bobbio, *Thomas Hobbes and the Natural Law Tradition*, trans. D. Gobetti (Chicago, 1993), 154–55; Ian Shapiro, *The Evolution of Rights in Liberal Theory* (Cambridge, 1986), 23.

12. Shapiro, *The Evolution of Rights in Liberal Theory*, 23.

13. Strauss, *Natural Right and History*. Page references to this work are given in parentheses in the text.

14. Hobbes, *Leviathan*, I, 15; ed. Oakeshott, 104–5.

15. For my own interpretation of what Locke has to say about natural law in the full range of his writings (and which is very much at odds with Strauss's reading), see Francis Oakley and Elliot W. Urdang, "Locke, Natural Law, and God," *Natural Law Forum* 11 (1966): 92–109, and Francis Oakley, "Locke, Natural Law, and God: Again," *History of Political Thought* 17 (1997): 624–51.

16. For the conflicted universe of Hobbes interpretation, see above, p. 31 and n. 33.

17. Thomas Rutherford, *Institutes of Natural Law*, 2nd ed. (Cambridge, 1774), 29–30, cited in Knud Haakonssen, "From natural law to the rights of man: a European perspective on American debates," in Michael J. Lacey and Knud Haakonssen, eds., *A Culture of Rights: The Bill of Rights in Philosophy, Politics, and Law, 1791 and 1991* (Cambridge, 1991), 19–61 (at 34).

18. Knud Haakonssen, *Natural Law and Moral Philosophy: From Grotius to the Scottish Enlightenment* (Cambridge, 1996), 6; cf. 61, where he states that "the history of Natural Law is to a significant degree a story of the continuities in moral thought, although providing a framework within which innovation took place."

19. Thus Haakonssen, *Natural Law and Moral Philosophy*, 61–62. Cf. idem, "The Moral Conservatism of Natural Rights," in Ian Hunter and David Saunders, eds., *Natural Law and Civil Sovereignty: Moral Right and State Authority in Early Modern Political Thought* (Basingstoke and New York, 2002), 27–42.

20. Strauss, *Natural Rights and History*, 198–99, n. 43. Cf. his succinct defence of the method in "On a Forgotten Kind of Writing," in his *What is Political Philosophy and Other Studies* (Chicago, 1959), 221–32. Taking a very different tack, and speaking of Locke as well as Hobbes, Shapiro, *The Evolution of Rights in Liberal Theory*, 275, argues that "the importance they ascribed to the subject of rights and individual consent was not seen as threatening to their beliefs in objective [moral] standards of value and interest."

21. See above, chapter 1, 31–32, and n. 33.

22. Strauss, *Natural Right and History*, 163–65.

23. Villey, "La genèse du droit subjectif chez Guillaume d'Occam," 126; cf. idem, *La Formation de la pensée juridique moderne,* 4th ed. (Paris, 1975), 225.

24. Thus, stressing Ockham's preoccupation with the absolute power of God and his concomitant voluntarism, his dismantling of the Aristotelian teleological physics, and his reduction of both the natural and social worlds to aggregates of particulars, de Lagarde argues that the "natural right" which he seeks to safeguard is "a subjective individual right" and that for him, the natural law amounts, accordingly, to nothing other than "a sum of natural rights" (*La Naissance de l'esprit laïque au déclin du moyen âge,* 2nd ed., 5, esp. 44, 78, 118, 284–88; see also the 1st ed., 6, esp. 163–85). De Lagarde's approach was later taken up and explored further by Louis Vereeke, "Individu et communauté selon Guillaume d'Ockham (+ 1349)," *Studia moralia* 9 (No. 3, 1965), 150–77.

25. Isaiah Berlin, "Two Concepts of Liberty," in his *Four Essays on Liberty* (Oxford, 1969), 129, n. 1; Heinrich Rommen, "The Genealogy of Natural Rights," *Thought* 29 (1954): 403–25 (at 415–20); Dumont, *Essays on Individualism,* 62–66; Bastit, *Naissance de la loi moderne,* 234, 244, 298, 301. The attention of others in the Anglophone world was drawn to Villey's claim via Martin P. Golding, "The Concept of Rights: A Historical Sketch," in Elsie L. Bandman and Bertram Bandman, eds., *Bioethics and Human Rights* (Boston, 1978), 44–50.

26. Stretching, so far as the issue of subjective rights is concerned from his "L'Idée du droit subjectif et les systèmes juridiques romains," *Revue historique de droit français et étranger,* ser. 4, 24 (1946): 201–27, to his restatement of his case in *Le droit et les droits de l'homme* (Paris, 1983). Villey presents his case for fourteenth-century origins succinctly and conveniently in his "La genèse de droit subjectif chez Guillaume d'Occam" and in his *La formation de la pensée juridique moderne,* 225–62. There are good (though critical) synoptic recapitulations of Villey's unfolding position in Tierney, *The Idea of Natural Rights,* 13–42, and in Reid, "The Canonistic Contribution to the Western Rights Tradition," 51–58.

27. Villey, "La genèse de droit subjectif chez Guillaume d'Occam," 127.

28. Thus Villey, "La genèse du droit subjectif chez Guillaume d'Occam," 103: "... cette philosophie dite du droit naturel classique ... ait été nécessairement exclusive du droit subjectif." And (126): "Les droits subjectifs des individus ont comblé le *vide* résultant de la perte du droit naturel." Interestingly enough, Luc Ferry and Alain Renaut, *From the Rights of Man to the Republican Idea,* trans. Franklin Philip (Chicago, 1992), 29–47, treat Villey as in some measure an ideological bedfellow with Strauss and, by extension, with Hannah Arendt and Martin Heidegger.

29. Tierney, *The Idea of Natural Rights,* 18; Reid, "The Canonistic Contribution to the Western Rights Tradition," 55–56.

30. Villey, "La genèse du droit subjectif chez Guillaume d'Occam," 98. Cf. 105, where he notes that the notion of subjective rights "résulte de l'association des deux idées de *pouvoir* et de *droit.*" Or, again, 109; "Tout *jus* a pour suite pratique l'exercice d'une *potestas.*"

31. De Lagarde, *Naissance de l'esprit laïque au déclin du moyen âge,* 2nd ed., 5:287 and 334.

32. Thus Tierney, *The Idea of Natural Rights,* 199, summarizing Villey, *La formation de la pensée juridique moderne,* 260–61.

33. William of Ockham, *Opus nonaginta dierum,* in R. F. Bennett and H. S. Offler, eds., *Guillelmi de Ockham: Opera politica,* 3 vols. (Manchester, 1940–56), 2, 373–858.

34. Villey, *La formation de la pensée juridique moderne,* 253 (cf. 261), and, for what follows, his "La genèse du droit subjectif chez Guillaume d'Occam," 120–27.

35. Villey, "La genèse du droit subjectif chez Guillaume d'Occam," 124.

36. Ibid.

37. For a negative appraisal of the likelihood of any such linkages, see Charles Zuckerman, "The Relationship of Theories of Universals to Theories of Church Government in the Middle Ages: A Critique of Previous Views," *Journal of the History of Ideas* 35 (1973): 579–94. For a less unsympathetic but cautious and carefully nuanced approach to the matter, see A. S. McGrade, "Ockham and the Birth of Individual Rights," in Brian Tierney and Peter Linehan, eds., *Authority and Power: Studies on Medieval Law and Government presented to Walter Ullmann on his Seventieth Birthday* (Cambridge, 1980), 149–65.

38. Villey, "La genèse du droit subjectif chez Guillaume d'Occam," 103–4; cf. idem. *La formation de la pensée juridique moderne,* 227–30. For contemporary approaches to the general issue, see Virginia Black, "On Connecting Natural Rights with Natural Law," *Persona y derecho* 22 (1990): 183–209.

39. Thus Jaques Maritain, *Les droits de l'homme et la loi naturelle* (Paris, 1942); Finnis, Aquinas: *Moral, Political, and Legal Theory,* esp. 132–38, 170–76.

40. Though more than one view can be taken about what, precisely, he meant by that language. See Tierney, *The Idea of Natural Rights,* 193–203; Brett, *Liberty, Right and Nature,* 49–87.

41. See above, chapter 3, 75–80.

42. Even, interestingly enough, by de Lagarde, *La Naissance de l'esprit laïque,* 2nd ed., 4:52, and 5:269, where, referring to Gratian's great twelfth-century *Concord of discordant canons* (*Decretum*), he noted that in his ecclesiological writings Ockham had "installed himself in the labyrinth of the *Decretum* and its glosses." For Ockham's extensive use of the canon law, the extent and limits of his knowledge of it, and the precise sources he may have used, see S. Gagner, "Vorbemerkungen zum Thema 'Dominium' bei Ockham," *Miscellanea medievalia* 9 (1974): 293–327; Brian Tierney, "Ockham, the Conciliar Theory, and the Canonists," *Journal of the History of Ideas* 15 (1954): 40–70; idem, "Natural Law and Canon Law in Ockham's *Dialogus,*" in J. G. Rowe, ed., *Aspects of Late Medieval Government and Society: Essays Presented to J. R. Lander* (Toronto, 1986), 3–24.

43. Tuck, *Natural rights theories,* 5–15.

44. Harold J. Berman, *Law and Revolution: The Formation of the Western Legal Tradition* (Cambridge, MA, 1983), e.g., 226–30.

45. Tuck, *Natural rights theories,* 13–15. Admittedly, Tuck's presentation is not always clear or consistent. For a probing critique, see Brian Tierney, "Tuck on Rights: Some Medieval Problems," *History of Political Thought* 4 (1983): 429–41.

46. It would be easy to get the impression, indeed, that the only people to have raised the possibility of the existence of rights talk in the medieval centuries are Villey and Tuck.

47. For what follows I am almost entirely dependent on the detailed discussions of the matter in Tierney, *The Idea of Natural Rights* and Reid,

"The Canonist's Contribution to the Western Rights Tradition." But cf. Janet Coleman, "Medieval Discussions of Human Rights," in Wolfgang Schmale, ed., *Human Rights and Cultural Diversity* (Goldbuch, 1993), 103–119.

48. Reid, "The Canonistic Contribution to the Western Rights Tradition," 59 (italics mine). Taking canonistic matrimonial law as a powerful illustration of this claim, he explores it from 72 to 91.

49. *Decretum Magistri Gratiani,* D. 1, *dictum ante* cap. 1 and cap. 1, in *Corpus Juris Canonici,* ed. A. Friedberg, 2 vols. (Leipzig, 1879–81), 1:2.

50. Tierney, *The Idea of Natural Rights,* 65–66.

51. Tierney, *The Idea of Natural Rights,* devotes no less than a hundred pages to Ockham and the Franciscans. Cf. Paolo Grossi, "Usus facti. La nozione di proprietà nella inaugurazione dell'età nuova," *Quaderni Fiorentini per la storia del pensioro giuridico moderno* 1 (1972): 287–355.

52. For the ideal of apostolic poverty and a brief account of the dispute, see Francis Oakley, *The Western Church in the later Middle Ages* (Ithaca and London, 1979), 44–46, 155–56, 168.

53. Ockham, *Opus nonaginta dierum,* cap. 14, 28, 60, 61 and 62; in Bennett and Offler, eds., *Guillelmi de Ockham: Opera politica,* 2: 432–33, 492–93, 556, 561–62, 564–65. See the analysis of these and related texts in Tierney, *The Idea of Natural Rights,* 157–69.

54. Going so far, indeed, as to weave together "the idea of natural rights inherent in all persons with the specifically Christian concept of evangelical liberty...understood as a sphere of personal autonomy." Thus Tierney, *The Idea of Natural Rights,* 186.

55. A good sense of the complexity of this process of transmission down through the late medieval and early modern periods, and of the difficulty of constructing any one agreed historical account of how exactly it happened can be gleaned from a comparison of the differing versions proffered by Tuck, *Natural Rights Theories,* Brett, *Liberty, Right, and Nature,* and Tierney, *The Idea of Natural Rights.*

56. In what follows, I draw on Francis Oakley, "Legitimation by Consent: The Question of the Medieval Roots," *Viator* 14 (1983): 303–35, reprinted in idem, *Politics and Eternity: Studies in the History of Medieval and Early-Modern Political Thought* (Leiden, Boston, and

Cologne, 1999), 96–137. Also idem, "Disobedience, Consent, Political Obligation: The Witness of Wessel Gansfort (c. 1419–1489)," *History of Political Thought* 9, no. 2 (1988): 211–21, and Patrick Riley, *Will and Political Legitimation: A Critical Exposition of Social Contract Theory in Hobbes, Locke, Rousseau, Kant, and Hegel* (Cambridge, MA, 1982); idem, "How Coherent is the Social Contract Tradition?" *Journal of the History of Ideas* 34, no. 4 (1973): 543–62.

57. Note especially the use the canonists made of the Roman legal principles *Quod omnes tangit ab omnibus approbetur* and *plena et sufficiens potestas*. See Oakley, *Politics and Eternity*, 109–12.

58. Riley, "How Coherent is the Social Contract Tradition?" 561. See the same article (549–53) for the lack of clarity attaching to the notion of will in all the great contract theorists with the exception of Kant.

59. Thus Ewart Lewis, *Medieval Political Ideas*, 2 vols. (London, 1954), 1:160, where she adds: "Thus the consent on which [that] authority rested could not be construed as the free choice of self-determining wills — with an open alternative, perhaps of continuing in primitive anarchy." For a very different take on what consent may have involved in the later Middle Ages and a greater willingness to downplay the difference between medieval and early modern views, see Brian Tierney, *Religion, law, and the growth of constitutional thought: 1150–1650* (Cambridge, 1982), esp. 29–53.

60. Referring here to the writings of the English Separatists and of the Levellers, see Oakley, *Politics and Eternity*, 131–37.

61. Note Shapiro's claim (*The Evolution of Rights in Liberal Theory*, 273) that "there is a distinctive way of conceiving of individual rights that has been central to the Anglo-American tradition of political theory since the mid-seventeenth century, and that is very much alive in it today."

62. Michael Oakeshott, *Rationalism in Politics and Other Essays* (New York, 1962), 249.

63. The words cited are those of Haakonssen, "The Moral Conservatism of Natural Rights," in Hunter and Saunders, *Natural Law and Civil Sovereignty*, 27–42 (at 28), and idem, "From natural law to the rights of man," in Lacey and Haakonssen, eds., *A Culture of Rights*, 20–21. In Haakonssen's view it was David Hume and Adam Smith

who eventually transformed the rights theory and ushered in "moral conventionalism" ("The Moral Conservatism of Natural Rights," 28). Cf. Shapiro, *The Evolution of Rights in Political Thought,* 233–37; Janet Coleman, "The History of Political Thought in the Modern University," *History of Political Thought* 21 (2000): 152–71 (esp. 153–56).

Epilogue

1. I have in mind here the Collingwood of *The Idea of Nature* not the Collingwood who, in his role as expert on the history of Roman Britain, contributed a distinguished volume to the Oxford History of England. The Oxford philosopher Michel Foster (1903–1959) is well nigh forgotten today, but not entirely. For some of his pertinent writings and a series of recent appraisals of the significance of his contribution to the history of ideas, see Cameron Wybrow, ed., *Creation, Nature, and Political Order in the Philosophy of Michael Foster (1903–1959)* (Lewiston: Edwin Mellen Press, 1992).

2. Hobbes, *Leviathan,* ed. Oakeshott, Introduction, xi.

INDEX